CHRISTIANITY: ITS NATURE
AND ITS TRUTH

CHRISTIANITY ITS NATURE AND ITS TRUTH

BY

ARTHUR S. PEAKE, D.D.

PROFESSOR OF BIBLICAL EXEGESIS IN THE UNIVERSITY OF MANCHESTER

DESORMAIS

LONDON

DUCKWORTH & CO.

3 HENRIETTA STREET, COVENT GARDEN

1908

Published . . . . *October, 1908*
Second Impression, November, 1908
Third Impression, December, 1908

PREFACE

IT has long been the writer's conviction that more ought to be done to expound the truths of Christianity and the grounds on which they may still be accepted. The task is especially urgent for the sake of the young people in our churches, who are slipping away from the faith because they have been trained neither to understand nor to defend it. The present volume is intended as a modest contribution to this object. It should be judged in the light of its aim. It is addressed to those who are willing to read a discussion of the deepest things, provided that it is simple and popular in its treatment, and avoids the abstruse and technical. Much has accordingly been omitted which must have found a place in a formal treatise on Systematic Theology and Apologetics, while even in the subjects discussed some aspects have been ignored as inappropriate to those for whom the volume is primarily designed. It was also necessary, for the same reasons, to restrict the size of the book, and several chapters have been left out that readers might not be repelled by its length. While many of the topics discussed are matters of controversy among Christian people, care has been taken to exclude those subjects on which the lines of theological coincide with the lines of denominational cleavage. And while the author has not hesitated to express his own conviction on matters of debate, he trusts that he has not wounded the feelings of those who take a different view.

Considerable portions of the volume have appeared in *The Sunday Strand*, but they have been revised and expanded, and several new chapters have been added. The author has received so many requests for their republication, enforced by assurances of the help which they have given, that he trusts they may contribute in their completer form to a firmer grasp and clearer perception of the nature and the truth of the vital facts and principles on which Christianity depends for its very existence.

CONTENTS

CHAPTER I

WHAT IS RELIGION?

CHAPTER II

HAS THEOLOGY HAD ITS DAY?

CHAPTER III

WHY I CANNOT BE A MATERIALIST

CHAPTER IV

IS THERE A GOD?

CHAPTER V

WHICH IS THE BEST RELIGION?

CHAPTER VI

THE TRINITY IN UNITY

CHAPTER VII

SIN

Contents

CHAPTER VIII

DOES IT MATTER IF THE GOSPEL HISTORY IS UNTRUE ?

CHAPTER IX

CAN WE TRUST THE GOSPEL PORTRAIT OF JESUS ?

CHAPTER X

THE MIRACLES OF JESUS

b

CHAPTER XI

THE SUPERNATURAL BIRTH OF JESUS

CHAPTER XII

THE RESURRECTION OF JESUS

CHAPTER XIII

THE DIVINITY OF CHRIST

Contents

CHAPTER XIV

THE PROBLEM OF THE INCARNATION

CHAPTER XV

THE WORK OF CHRIST

CHAPTER XVI

PERSONAL SALVATION

CHRISTIANITY
ITS NATURE AND ITS TRUTH

CHAPTER I
WHAT IS RELIGION?

TO the question, "What is Religion?" many
answers are given. One will say that religion
consists in going to church and participating in certain acts of worship. Another will contend that
religion is rather an intellectual attitude towards the
universe, and consists essentially in what a man believes. While the former identifies religion with the
cultus or worship, the latter identifies it with the creed.
A third, however, will insist that the main thing in
religion is conduct. Whether a man is religious or not
depends on whether he is upright or not. Now, it is
true that religion is closely associated with all of these,
with cultus, creed, and conduct. The first two are its
direct creation, and the latter has been largely influenced by it. Yet religion in its innermost nature is
not any of these things at all.

Without attempting a scientific definition, I may
sufficiently describe my view by saying that religion is

B

fellowship with the Unseen. Man's nature bears upon it the hall-mark of heaven. Woven into its very texture we discover a faculty for which the material universe does not prepare us. Our physical senses find their exercise and satisfaction in the physical world, to which they are exquisitely adjusted. But man has always manifested the impulse to pass behind the veil of the visible and penetrate into the unseen, and this tendency demonstrates to us the reality of the invisible order. The things of time press in upon us through every channel of the senses ; we are conscious of them every moment in joy or pain, in desire or gratification, in sight and sound, in labour or rest. We cannot escape from them, their innumerable waves beat on the shore of consciousness at every point. Were it not that we train ourselves to select from our impressions those which appeal to our interest, and to ignore the rest, the strongest brain would quickly be distracted and lose all power of control. But as it is, the outward world clamours at every gate of our physical being, forces itself on our notice, and demands our constant attention. Yet what lifts us above the world is that we do not suffer ourselves to be captured and absorbed by it. The prison walls may close about us, but our prison is open to the sky. Thither our spirits aspire for their contentment, and in its possession our deepest happiness is to be won. Born into a tangible world, and linked intimately to it by the structure of our being, we yet bear within us the seed of the Divine. If on the one side man is the fellow of the beast, on the other he is sprung from the race of flame. Driven out of himself and beyond the world, he seeks his rest in communion with the Unseen. True to the deepest impulses of his being, he creates religion.

Now the experience he thus achieves is in the heart of it emotional. However justly we may criticise Schleiermacher's famous description of religion as feeling, and especially as a feeling of dependence, I do not doubt that he put his finger on the right place when he found in feeling the essence of religion. Other elements enter it of necessity, but here we are at the centre. It is the meeting of spirit and spirit, the flush of happiness, the thrill of satisfaction, the sense of peace, the glad realisation that now at last a hunger, keener than hunger, has been appeased by the heavenly bread. God and the soul have met, and in the shock of that meeting there has come to the soul a wholly new emotion. There are things for which we pine, and no substitute will suffice. Perhaps the heart aches for a friend, and no other friend will assuage the bitter longing for the absent. Or it may think with a great desire of its old home and its native land, and no other scene can steal the yearning from it. So not even our dearest can meet the spirit at the depth where God meets it, and fill it with the sweet sense of contentment and repose. And the yearning of the spirit is a home-sickness for God.

Religion is that blessed experience in which man comes home to God, and with a happy smile sinks to rest in His embrace. True, the experience varies indefinitely in different people, since temperament, spiritual privilege, culture are at such different levels. In some it may express itself in an almost delirious rapture or wild orgiastic enthusiasm, while others may be awed into a great stillness, with their hearts full of a joy too deep for words or tears. And between extremes of this kind lie other ranges of feeling, but in all cases where religion does its work emotion must be the very core of the experience.

We may reverently believe that the crying out of heart and flesh for the living God can never have been unheeded by Him, who did not leave Himself without a witness in the human soul. Even in the most degraded races, where religion seems all of a piece with the disgusting savagery of their general life, we find a passion and an intensity which point to the deeply-felt desire, and to the experience of some response. If Christians put into their religion as much fervour as many of these lower races put into theirs, we should soon see the temperature of our Churches rising towards boiling point. Naturally the emotion generated is deeply contaminated with baser passions. Only the eye of love could detect in these hideous surroundings the germ of a purer faith. The unrestrained licence, the cold-blooded cruelty, the fantastic ceremonies, would blind us to the inmost meaning, were we not ready to penetrate to it by imagination and loving sympathy. And an unprejudiced observer would be struck with the remarkable parallels he could find in the practices and beliefs of some Christian Churches.

It is sometimes urged as a reproach to the mission preacher that he works on the feelings of his audience. It is true, and it ought to be true. The revivalist who fails to do it has not learned the elements of his work. He cannot, indeed, now appeal to the sense of terror as his predecessor could. The almost universal disbelief among educated Protestants in a material hell-fire has certainly weakened the urgency of appeal. But probably the chief reason why the missioner has largely abandoned the appeal to terror is that he finds that it meets with very little response. In the widespread breakdown of belief with which we are at present confronted, very many have practically ceased to believe that, even if there should be a future life, they have anything to dread in it. This has not been clear gain ; for the solemn truth that there is such a thing as retribution, and that as a man sows he must reap, cannot slip from the popular consciousness without weakening the tension of the ethical standard. But neither has it been all loss, for, at least, it is better to win men by love ; and the appalling confidence with which men used to arrogate to themselves the right of asserting the destiny of their fellows shocks me profoundly as I look back upon it.

But while terror no longer holds its former place, it is quite true that emotionalism remains a potent weapon in the missioner's armoury. There could be nothing more absurd than the depreciation to which emotion is subjected, usually by cold-blooded pedants who aim to pass for superior persons. The emotional life lies at the very centre of our being, and it is the one thing that must be touched and captured if the man is to be fundamentally transformed. We must, of course, discriminate. The emotion of which I speak is no shallow sentiment ruffling the mere surface of our life. It is rather an experience in which the fountains of the great deep are broken up. No doubt emotion may be a dangerous thing to play with, and religious emotion most of all. Nevertheless the risk must be taken in many cases in order that a man may be, to use the old-fashioned expression, soundly converted at all. And this explains why it is that even the wildest excitement has often co-operated in achieving sterling results. Some natures cannot fuse except at a very high temperature ; and while many of us prefer that still intensity of feeling in which we think that the spiritual change is best achieved, we ought to be willing to become all things to all men if thereby we may save some. And even after the intellect has accepted the Gospel, and the will has bowed in subjection to it, there needs to be that passionate self-abandonment in which, with a glad thrill and shock of content, Divine and human blend, and the troubled spirit finds rest. Nothing can take the place of feeling, for without it the religious instinct misses its supreme satisfaction. It is not in thought, but in feeling, that we come nearest to God, whose name is Love. It is, then, no legitimate reproach to a missioner that his preaching is emotional. Only we must beware that emotion does not degenerate into sensationalism or mawkish sentimentalism.

It is not the precise form which the experience takes that matters. Even in those Churches which have cultivated a warm type of spirituality, and sedulously nourished the emotional side of religion, the type of manifestation changes in course of time. But it by no means follows that they are losing their central heat. It is, perhaps, more likely that the fire glows even more hotly because its heat is not flung off in such a shower of sparks. But whether this be so or not, it is our primary duty to guard the sacred fire. We need for each individual an original spiritual experience, the electric thrill of definite contact with God. In religion the second-hand is intolerable, yet how much religious life is the echo of an echo. And when we have caught the flame direct from God, with what jealous care we need to keep it burning! To dwell in the secret place of the Most High is the supreme method of the spiritual life. There we are warmed and fed, and there religion fulfils in us its perfect work.

But while the primary element in religion is emotion, its relation to theology and to the moral life is a question on which it is necessary to reach a decision, and the consideration of it will help to elucidate what has been already said. I pass on to discuss the relation between religion and morality.

There is a story told of Sam Jones, the American revivalist, which will perhaps serve to introduce this part of the subject. He was preaching to a camp-meeting of coloured people, and they were having an ecstatic time. Every face was bathed in rapture, every sentence was punctuated with hallelujahs. The preacher, however, who believed in a walk and conduct in harmony with the Gospel, became more and more practical in the treatment of his theme. And as he went on to speak, with great point and plainness, of such definite matters as chicken-stealing a change came over the assembly. Heads began to droop, the hallelujahs died down, and the preacher continued his discourse in a frigid silence. At last a grey-headed old negro could bear it no longer ; this was not what they had come for, so he stepped up behind the revivalist and said to him : " Brudder Jones, don't you think you're kinder putting a damper on the meeting?"

Why does this story strike us as it does ? It is because religion, as we understand it, leaves no room for chicken-stealing. Are we, then, to say that the camp-meeting was made up of hypocrites ? That would be wholly to misunderstand the situation. The worshippers would have been amazed and indignant had any one hinted that they had not " got religion," as the American phrase has it. And their surprise would not have been completely unjustified. A certain kind of religion they undoubtedly possessed— genuine, too, so far as it went. What explanation can we give of this attitude ?

All who have read the interesting but superficial and ill-informed chapter entitled " Religion Given " in Matthew Arnold's *Literature and Dogma* will remember that for him religion is simply " morality touched by emotion," that " the object of religion is *conduct*," and that " conduct is three-fourths of life." This is utterly wide of the mark. It would be as true to say of many religions that they are " immorality touched by emotion " ; and, indeed, they have often found their most congenial—nay, their supreme— expression in what would seem to us the most revolting vice. When we are determining the nature of religion and its relation to morality, it is imperative for us to keep these facts in view. The lower religions show us the religious instinct at work and help us to understand its meaning, and in the light of them it is clear that the definition " morality touched by emotion " is simply irrelevant. This is not true of savages only ; even in highly developed civilisations the same thing is constantly to be found. In Greece itself morality and religion were quite distinct ; virtue was the concern of the philosopher rather than of the priest.

The single correct element in Matthew Arnold's definition is the recognition of emotion. But the function he assigns to it is quite foreign to its intrinsic nature. He regards morality and religion as fundamentally the same thing ; the only difference is that when a deep feeling pervades morality or a glow of emotion enkindles it, we give to this transfigured morality the name of religion. The truth is that religion is not morality at all, but it is emotion. As I have previously defined it, it is fellowship with the Unseen. Now, when the unseen powers were themselves conceived as lustful, cruel, false, it would be folly to imagine that fellowship with them would have a moral character. Religion would be the sanction of men's passions rather than a restraint. And we know, as a matter of fact, that religion has in many instances worked for the moral degradation rather than for the uplifting of man. And even in the religions which have blended morality indissolubly with them—the Religion of Israel and Christianity—there is much that is simply unmeaning on Matthew Arnold's formula. There are other types of utterance than " Oh, how I love Thy Law ; it is my meditation all the day." That, of course, is both moral and religious. But suppose we take such a passage as this : " As the hart panteth after the water-brooks, so panteth my soul after Thee, O God." Or, again : " Whom have I in heaven ? and possessing Thee, I delight in nought upon earth." Surely these are religion of the purest kind. But what have they to do with morality or with the conduct that is three-fourths of life ? For religion there are two beings in the universe—God and the soul, the soul and its God. It would abide were there no other human being in the world ; it is independent of those conditions which make morality possible.

But, further, morality touched with emotion may have no religious character. There are many who would definitely exclude from their theory of the universe and from the conduct of their lives all belief in or reference to the unseen realities. Yet they may be fired with passionate enthusiasm for lofty ideals and generous actions. Their morality is saturated with emotion, but it has nothing to do with religion in the proper sense of the term.

Naturally, when one hits on Matthew Arnold's amazing discovery that the Old Testament conception of God was that of an Eternal not ourselves making for righteousness, a stream of tendency manifesting itself in history, it ought to occasion no surprise that the theory of religion should match it. The Hebrews, however, believed intensely in a personal God who bore a personal name, which probably did not mean " the Eternal " at all ; and for them religion was not a rule of conduct embraced with passion, but a passion for God Himself. It is, indeed, the great glory of the Religion of Israel and of Christianity that they have wedded morality and religion, so that the moral as well as the religious test is applied to a man's claim to be a genuine Christian or an Israelite indeed. That is one of the most wonderful things in all the world's history. But we see how wonderful it is only when we remember that through vast spaces of that history religion has been as likely to work against morality as for it. In the light of this we realise the unique glory of the revelation in the Bible : " This is the Lord's doing ; it is marvellous in our eyes."

When we look at the fundamental facts of human nature we are struck by the way in which these two forces often pull in opposite directions. Roughly, one might say that a large part of humanity is split into two classes—those in whom the ethical and those in whom the religious temper predominates. The tendency of the former is to distrust emotion, to dwell on its moral perils, its relaxing character, its lawless instincts. It looks with eyes of cold disapproval on the excesses of religion, from the wild dances of savage worship up to a red-hot Methodist prayer-meeting. To its grave, rigorous austerity these unrestrained outbursts of feeling are not merely uncongenial, but fraught with possibilities of moral disaster. On the other hand, the religious type of character looks on the ethical as cold, narrow, and hide-bound, as self-excluded from the supreme beatitude of life. And when we find the moral type becoming religious, or the religious following the strictest rule of morality, there is often a difference in the underlying motive. One will say, " I must do right at all costs, and I am religious because it is my duty to be so." The other will say, " Religion is my deepest need, and God is my highest good. I must be moral, for only so can I maintain my fellowship with my God and express in action the love I feel for Him." No doubt there are many whose natures are beautifully poised, where the moral and religious elements balance and blend. But probably in most people one tendency or the other is predominant. Yet let no one be discouraged because he feels himself to be defective on this side or that. We are not abandoned to nature, we live in the era of God's omnipotent grace. " On this side of the river and on that was the tree of life, bearing twelve *manner of* fruits, yielding its fruit every month : and the leaves of the tree were for the healing of the nations." Yes, if we feel that between the two types there runs in nature this broad and deep distinction, there are the leaves of healing on this side and on that.

So far, then, I have sought to vindicate the radical distinction between Religion and Morality. They spring from wholly different instincts in our nature, and are often found acting in antagonism, or viewing each other with mutual distrust and disdain. Morality is a thing of order and law ; its tendency is to enthrone decorum and respectability. Religion defies conventionality, and bursts the strait waistcoat in which propriety would fetter it. It is an explosive force. I often think of it as a kind of spiritual dynamite. It is incalculable in its movement : " Thou canst not tell whence it cometh or whither it goeth." It does not conform to precedent or confine itself to grooves, but cuts for itself the channel in which its hot lava runs. The contrast comes out clearly enough in the story of David and Michal. When David danced before the ark with all his might, he was utterly careless about the decorum of his conduct. It was not simply that it was indecorous for a king to act as he did. It is quite plain from the story that Michal felt his dancing to fall below the standard of decency which any respectable Hebrew would maintain. In her eyes David had acted as one of the vile fellows, to such a pass religious excitement had brought him. That is the verdict of Morality. David, so far from denying the accusation, glories in it : " For God's sake I will be yet more vile." Religious passion carries him past the bounds that austere morality would impose.

Religion and morality have each their due place in human life. And this creates the difficult problem of their adjustment. This is not to be effected through the absorption of one by the other. There are many who degrade religion into mere philanthropy, while others will see in it only a warmer morality. Many, again, make a fervent religion cover conspicuous moral deficiencies. But we must insist that each shall have its rights regarded and maintained. And since no satisfaction can be won while the soul is torn by conflicting tendencies, we must reach the point where they blend in perfect harmony. It is, as I have said before, peculiarly the achievement of the higher religion of Israel and of the Gospel to have effected this union with complete success. The Hebrew prophets were confronted with a religion that went hand-in-hand with pitiless oppression, with the denial or maladministration of justice, with shameless immorality. Some of them, like Amos, spoke to the conscience of the people, with the stern declaration that the righteousness of Israel's God would make Him merciless to the sin of His people. It was not in costly offerings, in splendid feasts, in gorgeous ceremonies or thrilling music that acceptable service must be rendered to Him. "I hate, I despise your feasts, and I will take no delight in your solemn assemblies. Yea, though ye offer me your burnt offerings and your meat offerings, I will not accept them: neither will I regard the peace offerings of your fat beasts. Take thou away from me the noise of thy songs, for I will not hear the melody of thy viols. But let judgement roll down as waters and righteousness as an ever-flowing stream." For Amos morality was the supreme worship that the nation rendered to God. It was so because he realised with such intensity the moral character of God. His message, it is true, needed to be supplemented on many sides. But he grasped with almost unparalleled power, and expressed with a clearness that left nothing to be desired, his fundamental axiom: The God of Israel is a righteous God, and demands righteousness in His people. The moralising of the Deity involves the moralising of the religion.

With Hosea the primary stress was not, as with Amos, on the ethical, but on the religious. For him the relation of Israel to God is supreme. It is the perversion of this which has brought moral evil in its train. It is because the nation has been untrue to the marriage troth, has forsaken Yahweh for the Baalim, that its life is so stained with vice and crime. But though the emphasis is placed differently by the two prophets, they both start from the same principle. The God of Israel is a moral Deity ; that can be no true religion of Israel which sanctions vice or is indifferent to righteousness. Their work was carried forward by their successors, who burnt the truth they proclaimed into the conscience of their people. And the flower of all this glorious development was Christianity. So completely did the Gospel fuse religion and morality into one that it often comes as a startling novelty to a man when he is told that the two are quite distinct. No higher tribute can be paid to the success with which they have been blended by Christianity.

Yet the clearness with which this is expressed in the Bible has not prevented the most astonishing deviation from its teaching among those who take it as their rule of life. Much of Christian history has been of the most painful and disappointing character. Largely, this must be accounted for by a very obvious consideration. The level of morality in the heathen world at the time when the Gospel first touched it was indescribably low. The new religion was planted in an uncongenial paganism, like leaven in the large mass of unleavened meal. Its external progress far outstripped the internal. The world became nominally Christian while it was heathen at its heart. The rate of advance was so slow, that retrogression rather than progress seemed often to be the result. Yet the tide moved forward, though the spent waves often appeared to be receding. Much has still to be done ere our civilisation is penetrated with the Christian spirit. But it is more and more recognised that on the one side no independent system of philosophy and no rival religion pitches the ethical standard so high as the Gospel; while, on the other hand, none gives such power to respond to the demand. A non-moral Christianity is a contradiction in terms.

But we ought not to be surprised, in the light of the analysis I have given, when we are confronted by the unhappy spectacle of a profession of religion accompanied by a low morality. The pious scoundrel, in the form of a fraudulent director or trustee, or a man convicted of drunkenness or immorality, is indeed a painful sight, a sore scandal to the Church and a reproach to religion. Yet he need not be a hypocrite. There are, no doubt, always specimens of the ancient class who devour widows' houses, and for a pretence make long prayers. But, quite apart from these, there are the people who have genuine religious feelings and desires, but combine with them a low moral standard. Partly this is due to the fact that they are much

c

more developed on the religious than on the ethical side. To some extent it is due to sheer blindness of perception. There were many holy people not long ago who thought that it was quite right to keep slaves. And I have heard of a director who was so religious that he would not read a newspaper on Monday because it had been printed on Sunday, who yet was responsible, with his colleagues, for a colossal financial disaster which plunged thousands into ruin. But we must also fall back on our principle of the radical distinction of Religion and Morality and the frequent antagonism between them in the lower stages of their development.

Religion convulses a man to the depths, and it is not strange that when the fountains of the great deep are broken up some very offensive mud should occasionally be stirred to the surface. It is the very strong sense of this which has contributed in many minds to the distrust of revivals. They dislike the crisis type of religion, prefer that conversion should be gradual and unexciting, pass through a given order, and be conducted regularly throughout.

What should our own attitude be in reference to this ? I think we cannot so far deny our deepest convictions as calmly to set aside the passionately emotional type of religion. Yet just because it is emotional, and passionately emotional, we must frankly recognise its moral perils and take precautions against them. A wise training in the moral life from the earliest years may root the ethical character so firmly that no gust of passion will hereafter be able to snap it. A steady insistence, as we preach religion, on the moral qualities that our religion demands may also prove a powerful safeguard. Above all, as we stimulate emotion let us guide it into ethical channels. Let it be clearly understood that, while on the one hand religion is the best creator of morality, on the other hand morality is necessary if the religious instinct is to receive its fullest satisfaction. It is only the holy who can realise that perfect fellowship with the Holy God in which the highest and purest bliss of religion is to be found.

But now I ask the question which presses on the mind of many : Is religion destined to be a permanent element in human life ? Few things are more impressive than this, that everywhere religion is characteristic of man. To me it is the sure promise that religion cannot die. The frequent assertions that there are tribes without religion are not endorsed by the most competent anthropologists, though the forms it assumes may seem, through their unfamiliarity, to have no definitely religious character. To the savage religion is often one of the main concerns of life, bound up with all his dearest interests and inseparable from all his activities. Its rites are fraught with energy of the most potent kind ; the powers with whom it brings him into contact are mighty to work him weal or bane. He jealously guards the sacred ceremonies from all that would profane them; the eye of the uninitiated may not see the holy mysteries, nor must his ear ever listen to the secret lore. Hence the traveller may know much of the ordinary life of a tribe, while he remains completely ignorant that it possesses a religion at all. Even after he has won its confidence, disarmed its suspicion, and thawed its reserve, he may still be excluded from knowledge of its religion. Again and again prolonged intimacy has discovered what for years had evaded the closest scrutiny, and the " irreligious " tribe has been found to possess a religion of a very elaborate kind.

Few things are more impressive than this, that everywhere religion is characteristic of man. To me it is the sure promise that religion must be a permanent element in human life. If it is said that with the repulsive and cruel heathenism of howling savages we can have nothing to do, since religion means such utterly different things in their case and ours, that is wholly to miss the point. If one were to say that hunger is not to be counted on as a permanent factor in the upward movement of the race because the feasts of the savage are so different from our own, the fallacy of such an argument would impose on no one. It is the same instinct in them and in us, though what is satisfaction to the one would inspire nothing but loathing in the other. What is important is, not that this or that type of food is taken, coarse and disgusting here, refined and delicate there, but that in

each case the same imperious craving makes itself
felt. And as with the hunger of the body so it is with
the hunger of the soul. In the breast of every man
this longing is implanted, the sense of need, the aspira-
tion for something higher to complete and crown his
life. It stings the spirit out of contentment with the
world, and bids it launch itself into the unknown. It
assures man that he is made for the infinite, that time
and space are not his measure, and can in no wise
meet his profoundest needs. It prophesies to him of
the unseen, and tells him that there he must seek the
springs which will slake his inward thirst.

Thus the crudity of man's earlier ideas, the repulsive nature of the practices through which the religious
instinct sought its gratification, must not blind us to
the essential meaning of the omnipresence of religion.
We do not judge the meaning of our physical faculties
by the random movements of the infant, his futile
efforts to satisfy the desires that stir within him, his
first stumbling attempts to walk, his first stammering
utterances. The vital thing, as we all know, is not
the expression of the instincts, but the fact that the
instincts are there. What promise they hold within
them becomes plain to us in after days when we see
the strong and sinewy athlete, or hang with delight
on the orator's words. And so with religion. Its
meaning is revealed to us not in its first blind gropings
after God, but in Christianity, its ultimate achievement. And just as little as we anticipate such a

development in the refinement of the satisfactions we give to our physical instincts as shall lead to the ultimate extinction of these instincts altogether, so little are we entitled to imagine that a time will come when man will outgrow his instinct for God. As surely as the one is a permanent part of our bodily, so surely is the other inextricably woven into the very texture of intellect and spirit. And this lies in the very conditions under which we live. However science unveils for us the secrets of the material universe, with whatever subtlety of research the psychologist drives his shafts into the bed-rock of human personality and brings to light the hidden thoughts and emotions of the unconscious or sub-conscious self, man will always remain what he essentially is, a finite being encircled and upheld by the Infinite, and slender will be all the store of his knowledge in comparison with the vast realm of mystery that is everywhere about him. The utmost he can do is to push back a little way on this side and on that the pall of darkness, and enlarge by so much the range of light. And so he will never lose the need for faith, or of dependence on the power that controls and sustains the world.

And so I return to the early history of religion. Nature in the higher realm is true to the law we find in the lower. Organism responds to environment ; the existence of the physical instinct is the guarantee that the means for its gratification are not lacking. How otherwise could the organ develop ? how could it, even if it came into existence ready-made, fail to perish through disuse ? We may think, then, of man, even at his lowest point, as illustrating this law in his spiritual life. Just as in the deep ocean the cuttle-fish throws out its groping tentacles on every side for food, since the senses of sight and hearing serve it less than the sense of touch, so we may think of the soul of man at the lowest blindly feeling for its spiritual satisfaction, and making tentative experiments on every side. In some directions experiments would result in disappointment, and gradually the attempts to win nourishment on these lines would be discontinued as fruitless. But inasmuch as the spiritual environment was always there to respond to the activities of the soul, experiments in other directions would be rewarded with success. Some glow would thrill through the spirit ; the light that lighteneth every man would be doing His beneficent work. Doing it, it may seem to us, at an almost inconceivably low level, stooping with Divine condescension to the depths. But the first step has been taken, which is the promise of all that is to follow ; religion is born into the world. Through what blind strugglings, what gross and revolting rites, what crass mythologies, it moved slowly upward, from crudity to refinement, from bloodthirsty cruelty to tenderness and humanity, it lies beyond my purpose to describe. The point I wish to emphasise is that the religious instinct was the universal agent in this great development, and that the instinct was met with stimulus and satisfaction by the living God, who planted it in man's breast. I do not refer only to that intense activity of God which we associate with the religions of revelation, where a special sensitiveness was developed on the one side and a special response was accorded to it on the other, culminating in the manifestation of the Son of God. Here God strikes more strongly into the current. But we must also confess that the first tiniest tricklings of the stream were not without His loving and watchful care. The random and feeble stretching of hands in dumb and barely conscious appeal did not pass unnoticed, nor was it noticed only to be despised. Some answer came to those prayers of weakness and ignorance, an answer that fostered the tiny spark of devotion.

It may seem to not a few that I am dealing with remote questions, with little bearing on the conditions which set us our practical problem. Even were that the case, I should still feel that I was justified in laying foundations even if they were sunk some distance below the surface. But what I have said seems to me to bear directly on one of the gravest issues which we are called to face. The impression is being industriously diffused that the day for religion is nearly done, and that it will soon be numbered with obsolete antiquities. Our own young people are exposed to this influence ; and what with skilful sapping and mining, and what with confident direct assault, faith is often in danger of collapse. Naturally the Christian case does not lend itself to brief demonstration, and the impatient temper can be catered for more easily by the telling proofs from the rationalistic side, that religion is a superannuated absurdity, than by the weaving of threads of argument into a reasoned justification for belief in Christianity. Yet there are some arguments that admit of being stated with cogency and brevity which are also singularly impressive in their character. And one of these is the proof from the universality of religion. What is universal in human experience may be justly inferred to be permanent. Moreover, on an evolutionary theory it seems difficult to escape the inference that the very existence of the religious instinct, and still more its invariable manifestation in all the life of man, proves the existence of a spiritual universe. Otherwise we should have the spectacle of a faculty brought into existence, gradually developing, persisting amid all change, and yet doing all this with no environment to which it could correspond. If that is inconceivable, then the existence and diffusion of religion prove conclusively that there is a spiritual universe, though the nature of that universe has to be more precisely determined in other ways.

And in view of these facts we may quietly bear the criticism that human conceit alone could imagine that between God and man there could be these intimate relations. It is urged that the insignificance of man precludes any thought so madly presumptuous as that the infinite and eternal God should enter into fellowship with him. Dweller in a world so tiny, that it is but as nothing in the vast universe ; with a life briefer than a pulse-beat of eternity ; weaker than the forces of his own little world beyond all comparison ; what is he that God should spend a second thought upon him ? Such an objection is telling, but far from conclusive. So far as the vastness of the universe goes, it is sufficiently met by the consideration that physical size is not a criterion of worth. Matter and mind are not to be named together as if they could be compared with each other. The mind of the weakest and most degraded of men is greater in intrinsic worth than the whole universe of unconscious matter. It stands nearer to God, the Supreme Mind ; and in virtue of this common element of thought and emotion is not wholly wanting in capacity for communion with Him. But it is not the material universe, perhaps, that causes the greatest difficulties. The teeming inhabitants of these other worlds—does not man dwindle into insignificance by their side ? But this is only the child's difficulty in another form : How can God listen to so many children all saying their prayers at the same time ? It is answered by a consideration of God's greatness. The Infinite can care for small as well as great ; His resources cannot be overtaxed. That He so cares for man as to prize communion with him is confirmed by the universal religious instinct, in which He reveals Himself as Spirit seeking fellowship with the spirit of man.

On the other hand, some may say : " If there is a God, why should I have anything to do with Him ? I have no wish to be religious ; and I will live my own life, independent of any higher Power." From the point we have reached, this cannot be so effectually dealt with as from the Christian standpoint. But it may at least be said that such a man is deliberately maiming his life. If we would live healthfully and happily, we must live in harmony with the law of our own being. Our ideal should be completeness, so that no side of our complex nature should be left unexercised. Many who readily admit this for the body and intellect, and patiently train them that proficiency may be attained, leave the spiritual life quite uncultivated. Now, if religion were a mere accident in human life, this might be defended. But its universal presence in humanity warrants our belief that it is part of the very constitution of man to be religious. The non-religious man, therefore, is incompletely human—deficient in the highest and best prerogative of our race. I do not speak here of his duty to be religious, but of the immeasurable loss to the man himself if he fails to be so. And this is loss, not only of development, but of the refreshment of spirit that religion gives. The inward freedom and contentment, the deep, untroubled peace and the rapturous joy, the sense of mastery, the uplifting communion—all these, which religion gives as no other power can, are but a part of what he loses. Even so the price is too high.

CHAPTER II

HAS THEOLOGY HAD ITS DAY?

FEW things are more familiar than the impatience with which many in our day regard theology. The man in the street looks at theological dogmas as so many brilliant efforts of word-spinners, and can scarcely think himself into the point of view of those who fought so tenaciously the battles of dogmatic definition in the great Councils. What he cares about, he will tell you, is not creeds, but conduct; not the decisions of Œcumenical Councils, but the Sermon on the Mount. Nor is this protest without a certain justification. Theology in the past has exposed itself to many of the criticisms that are now offered upon it. It has suffered from a tendency to excessive minuteness of definition, from a failure to confront its theories with the facts of Scripture and experience, from an academic seclusion which has kept it out of touch with life. It aimed too much at omniscience, and its charts of the spiritual universe were filled in with a precision and a wealth of detail which strikes us to-day as astonishing. There is much that, in the very nature of things, cannot be grasped by human intelligence,

on which, however, the theologians were unwilling to
confess ignorance. They were in danger of disguising
in a mist of fine-spun phrases their inability to expound the unintelligible.

Yet some things may be urged in arrest of this
judgment. In the first place I think that the impatience of theology is largely exaggerated. It is a
significant fact that when some great theological
problem is being discussed in the pulpit or in fiction
a very widespread interest is at once excited. However the hearers may applaud a public speaker who
denounces theology in favour of a social or ethical
gospel, it is remarkable how keen is the attention
aroused by the discussion of these questions. The
attendance in our churches may be far from what we
could desire, yet religion is the only topic that could
draw together week by week the multitudes who are
found in our places of worship. And as to the criticisms of the man in the street, one could, indeed, wish
that the Sermon on the Mount really held the place
in his life which he fondly assigns to it ; but, quite
apart from that, he does not stand so aloof from
creeds and dogma as he himself imagines. Pope's
famous couplet, which relegates to graceless zealots
disputes on dogma, and affirms that " he can't be
wrong whose life is in the right," probably expresses
what he supposes himself to believe, yet he is, no
doubt, much more interested in discussions on theology
than he is himself aware.

In the next place such impatience with theology as is manifested must not be wholly put down to the account of the theologians. It is partly due to the mental habit of our own time. Whether it is the rush of life, that leaves men no time to think, or whether it is the flabbiness of a mind fed only on the newspaper and light literature, or the drugging of intellectual tastes by the thirst for pleasure and excitement, the ominous facts admit of no denial. Our age has lost the secret of meditation ; it is impatient of brooding thought. It is incapable of sustained mental exercise ; it flits like a butterfly from one thing to another ; its interests are alert, but they are easily fatigued. It is not theology alone which suffers from this, but the deep and serious treatment of all intellectual themes. Yet I am sure that there are very many who have escaped the mental demoralisation of which I have spoken, and who will welcome a serious attempt to expound in plain language the deep things of God. They are not afraid to face the task of thinking God's great thoughts after Him, if only they can be brought face to face with the essential truth and not be compelled to penetrate through a jargon of technical terms to the secret that lurks at the centre.

And while it must be frankly confessed that theology has been too much given to abstractions and to hairsplitting, yet even here we must beware of off-hand judgments. The plain man is prone to regard certain

doctrines as mere verbal puzzles or subtle quibbles.
Yet more accurate knowledge will show that what
seems to be a distinction without a difference may be
of vital significance. A razor edge may divide the
two, but it is, perhaps, a watershed that determines
the direction in which the great river of thought is to
run. How contemptuous the man in the street would
be of ecclesiastics contending over the " homoousion "
and the " homoiousion "—the question whether the
Son was " of the same essence " or " of like essence "
with the Father. " Christendom rent over a diph-
thong ! " he exclaims in scorn. Yet the scorn might
be reserved for a worthier object, since the question
at issue in the Arian controversy was this : Is Christianity to remain a monotheism or to become a new
paganism ? And frequently it will be found that
questions which on the surface seem devoid of all
practical importance are really matters of the most
serious practical concern.

Nor is there any real warrant for an outcry against
the abstruseness of theology. When everything has
been done to make things simple, the fact remains
that we live in a complex and mysterious universe.
Nothing is gained by simplification at the cost of
fidelity to truth, and it is not always by any means
a recommendation to a view that every element of
obscurity has been eliminated from it. It is good for
us to be baffled in our quest, to learn the limits of our
power, to be humbled by the vision of the vast ocean

of truth, to be awed by the sense of mystery. I am myself all for lucidity of statement where that can be rightly attained, but I do not forget that there is such a thing as a profane lucidity which has lost all sense of mystery. It is easy in our blindness to become intellectual Pharisees and pride ourselves on the narrow formula into which we have succeeded in packing the universe. What, we may truly ask, would any account of the Infinite be worth to us which professed to level it down to the comprehension of our finite intelligence ? A God whom we could wholly understand would be no God for us. It is not mystery from which we need to shrink, but something that is at times confounded with it.

There are some theologians who have gloried in the irrational. Their motto is, " I believe it because it is absurd," the phrase in which Tertullian boasted of the sacrifice of the intellect. But we must beware of identifying the mysterious with the irrational. A religion that did not transcend the reach of our unaided reason and demand our faith would be without value to us. But a religion that contradicted reason would be simply incredible. They are no true friends of the Gospel who divorce faith from the intellect, and that way the renunciation of faith ultimately lies. And we must also beware of confounding mystery with confused and incoherent thinking. Many a man has won a credit for depth when his thought was merely muddy.

I proceed, then, to give my reasons for the high estimate I place on theology and for my conviction that it will remain a permanent element in human thought.

Since it is by the very impulse of our nature that we seek from the tangled threads of emotions and ideas to weave an ordered and luminous pattern of that spiritual universe in which we have our being, I do not hesitate to assert that theology and religion are inseparably welded together. It needs, indeed, no reflection to convince us that so long as religion exists theology cannot cease to be, for religion is a certain experience involving a particular attitude to the universe which contains within it an implicit theology. So long as we remain reasonable beings we must reflect on our experience and seek to understand it ; we cannot permanently remain content with the incoherent and the unanalysed; we must sort and sift our impressions and ideas, introduce order into them, and bring system out of the chaotic mass. We must seek to understand religion as an organic and connected whole. The practical side cannot content us, we must have a theory of it. I can well understand if vague and random thinking were better than thinking which was clear, logical, and accurate, and if no thought at all were better than either, that then we ought to renounce any attempt to co-ordinate the facts of religious experience into a rational theory. But if it is an irrepressible instinct within us to win an ordered

D

apprehension of the facts of life, to pass from vagueness to definiteness, from obscurity to lucidity, from a disordered jumble to beautiful harmony, then the fact of religion forces upon us the duty of a theology. And since we have reason to believe in the permanence of religion, we may safely argue that theology will not die.

I have, it is true, argued that the essence of religion lies in feeling. In its widest application it may be defined as fellowship with the Unseen. Religion for the Christian is fellowship with God in Christ. It is the sense of utter dependence, of glad surrender, of confident trust, of blessed communion, of self-renouncing love. It finds its most characteristic expression in rapturous ecstasy, or in deep, unruffled peace. But while the glowing core of religion is this deep and passionate emotion, it is not an emotion directed towards the vague or the unknown. I could not deny to that feeling which stands in awe before this dark and wonderful universe the name of religion. The thrill of cosmic emotion, the sense of fellowship with Nature, and through Nature with the great underlying power that it expresses, is an experience of which one would not speak lightly.

But how different that is from the religion of the Christian who realises that the power which manifests itself in Nature is a self-conscious Person, a holy Will, a loving Father, a redeeming God! The very quality of the religious experience and its intensity and depth

depend upon the views we entertain as to the cha
of that Power with whom religion brings us
fellowship. "With *whom*," I say, and not "w
which"; and yet the distinction between the two,
which makes all the difference to the emotion, is the
intellectual belief in the personality of God.

It must be clearly understood that in pleading that
we shall not treat theology as an incubus of which
religion would do well to be rid I am not taking the
point of view of those who say that a system of theology is settled for us by revelation, and that we are
not to exercise upon it our own reflective faculties.

There is a religious attitude which is well illustrated
by the following story. A friend of mine went into a
church at a south-coast watering-place. In the course
of his sermon the preacher said: "Few things, my
friends, have done more harm in this world than
thought." He then proceeded, though it was surely
quite unnecessary: "Don't, my dear friends, put me
down as a thinker, put me down as a believer."

What, one may ask, is the value of belief without
thought? It is not belief in the highest sense, it is
superstition, it is the acceptance of things on authority
and tradition, such as might be found in a heathen
religion, where a man refuses to accept the arguments
of the missionary with the stolid reply that what was
good enough for his fathers is good enough for him.
Where would any higher religion have been to-day?
Where would our own religion be had it not been for

thinkers who were not content with tradition and authority?

What lies at the basis of this pestilent talk about the mischief of thought is the feeling that the intellect is a corrosive agent, which, if it be allowed to have its freedom, will eat out the belief in God and the spiritual order. Now, it is true enough that in many instances the intellect does work that way; but the cure for this is not to drug the reason, but to stimulate it to probe more deeply. It is surely a kind of atheism to distrust the intellect so radically, for what kind of a god would he be who furnished man for his journey to the Eternal with so misleading a guide? If the unfettered reason speaks with an atheistic voice, we may as well throw up our case at once.

The preacher would, I suppose, explain that the Bible has taught us quite clearly what we ought to believe, and that we ought not to allow a critical intellect to play on the utterances of the Holy Ghost. Where God has spoken, it is man's wisdom to be dumb. It is quite plain, however, that the great systematic theologians, while they have shared that point of view, have not felt themselves debarred from thinking on the truths of revelation. The labour they have devoted to them might be truly called colossal, and whether we agree with them or not, we cannot deny them the praise of vast learning and intellectual power. The question, however, arises for us whether the task of theology is simply to correlate the data given in

Scripture. It is quite obvious that Scripture itself is not a systematic theology. But, on the other hand, it is, I think, also true that we do not go to Scripture alone for the raw material out of which our theological fabric is to be woven. It is clear enough that this has often been consciously recognised. The schoolmen built not on Scripture only, but also on Aristotle; and it is plain that any systematic theology, for our own time, if it is to be adequate, must take into account a very large number of factors.

It is, no doubt, a sense of this which has led many to feel that constructive theology is almost beginning its work rather than bringing it to a close. The great articles of faith may remain, but a clearer understanding of them may be possible. We may understand their inter-relations, we may enrich our conceptions, make them less abstract and more vivid and concrete, carry them from the musty atmosphere of the museum into the open air, bring them more into contact with practical life. We may be willing to be more ignorant than our predecessors would confess themselves to be, simply because we understand better the complexity of the problems and the limitations of our powers. We may freely recognise that they suffered from an overweening self-confidence, from a resolution to leave nothing unexplained; we may renounce their tendencies to hair-splitting and minute precision, and be willing to leave a larger area of mystery, and to acknowledge that there are things which should lie in the shadows rather than be brought into the glare of broad day. If we have learnt modesty and humility, if we confess ourselves often baffled by the unknown, if we admit more heartily than theologians have often admitted that God's thoughts are higher than our thoughts and His ways past finding out, then religion and morality stand alike to gain.

Some time ago I was looking with some friends at a mediæval map of the world, and it was very interesting to see how inaccurate the author's conception of geography was. A liberal theologian, turning to another of rigid orthodoxy, said to him: " That's just about where we are in theology." Now, we need share neither the standpoint which excited the remark nor the disgust which the remark inspired, and yet recognise an instructive element in the story. For the older systematic theologians everything was mapped out with complete precision. They understood not only the broad outlines of ocean and continent, but every little creek and inlet was definitely marked on their theological maps. I think that most of us would be willing to admit that they went altogether too far in the direction of omniscience. And this feeling need not be based wholly on the belief that they sought to attain the unattainable ; it may rest much more on the conviction that there are many elements in the problem of which they took no account at all. They were speculating on disastrously imperfect data, and their construction was likely to be faulty.

The theologian of to-day will not, if he is wise, despise the past; he will recognise that intellectual giants, such as Origen or Augustine, Scotus Erigena or Thomas Aquinas, Calvin or Schleiermacher, cannot have deeply pondered on the Christian facts and doctrines without having said much that is worthy of the most respectful attention. He may profoundly disagree with much that they have to say, but he will at least be the better for knowing that they have said it and for understanding why he does not agree with them. At the same time, he will recognise that, for good or ill, we live in our own age and not in theirs, and that the scientific temper and outlook have made things very different for us.

The simple fact that the Ptolemaic conception of the physical universe has given place to the Copernican has profoundly modified the older conception of the world. Then how great a difference has been made by the wide acceptance of a far-reaching theory of evolution, not necessarily in this or that particular form! These are changes which affect our whole intellectual outlook, including religion and theology.

Once more, the demand for an ethical Gospel is perfectly valid in itself. Religion that does not sanction and inspire morality can command no allegiance from us to-day. But it would be easy to show that religion depends for its ethical power very largely on theology. Were the theological element to disappear from Christianity, it would be found, in the long run, that much of its moral power had disappeared with it. It is certainly no answer to this to point out that there are many who have abandoned the theology of the Gospel whc have retained its morality. A flower does not lose its beauty and fragrance the moment it is cut from its root, but give it time and the living power which it holds within itself will quickly dwindle when its contact with the earth is severed. And so the moral life of those who have abandoned Christianity has often been drawn from the Christian soil in which it first sprang up. The question is whether, sooner or later, the logic of the situation will not work itself out, and Christian ethics go the way of Christian theology. Indeed, the forecast that the surrender of the one would, in the long run, involve the surrender of the other is in the way of being verified. It is to be hoped that this will give some pause to the reckless utterance which we too often hear to the effect that doctrine is effete and that preaching must be simply ethical.

Moreover, we must not forget that the individual is largely controlled in his conduct and outlook by the social atmosphere in which he lives, and that to an extent far greater than he is aware, so that the natural impulses are checked by the moral and intellectual influences which are all the time playing upon and moulding him. Now, this atmosphere, though far from what we could wish it to be, is nevertheless saturated with Christian ideas, and the social influence

of Christianity thus remains active long after its
influence in the individual seems to have dwindled to
nothing. The question is not what will happen in a
single generation, but what is to happen in the long
run. Intellectually, the civilisation of Europe broke
with paganism many centuries ago, but, morally, that
civilisation has not even yet succeeded in working out
its pagan leaven. Hence, were Christianity to be
universally abandoned, it might still take many generations before the effects of that surrender would work
themselves out to their ultimate issues. I would also
remind those who are impatient of theology, but are
enthusiasts for conduct, that action is often mis-
directed because there is no clear grasp of principles ;
whereas, on the other hand, it is the man of ideas who
has often effected the most powerful changes in life.
Luther brooded in his cell on the problem of the
sinner's standing with God, and he convulsed Europe
as the result of his meditation. And, lastly, I would
urge that the root of much unbelief or uncertainty
lies in the fact that people do not understand their
own religion. Often they have mistaken some cari-
cature of the Gospel for the Gospel itself. And he
who would commend Christianity to our perplexed
and distracted age must himself understand the religion for whose acceptance he pleads.

And this has a practical relation to the pulpit.
There is more staying power in a ministry which gives
theology an important place than in a ministry which

lives from hand to mouth, to which the last nine days,
wonder is the breath of life. It is not theology that
has wearied people ; it is the insufferable tediousness,
the dry-as-dust pedantry with which it was often
presented that has wearied out the patience of the
longsuffering hearer. There is always room for a
ministry which will patiently and sympathetically
unravel the tangle of men's thoughts on the deepest
things. For men do think on them even if they have
ceased to look for light from the Church, which has
not been willing to come down to their platform,
assuming, as is its wont, too much faith in its audiences.

CHAPTER III

WHY I CANNOT BE A MATERIALIST

IT is not hard to understand why materialism should be so popular. In the first place, in our ordinary experience we are all the time made aware of sensations which seem to prove to us the existence of a material universe. Along all the avenues of the senses there stream into our consciousness impressions which we refer to the material world around us. Sight and sound, taste and smell and touch—these bring us, in all our waking moments, into conscious contact with the external world. Little can appear more actual to us than the objects about us. The solid earth under our feet, the starry sky above, the works of nature, and the constructions of man seem to us the most undeniable realities. We act invariably on the assumption that our senses give us a true report, and that the things which we see and touch are actually there. Now, this unceasing stream of impressions has a tendency to swamp the impressions of a subtler and less tangible kind. And since in ordinary life by far the greater proportion of our attention is directed to

43

material objects, it is not unnatural that many should come to forget that in the intangible order there may be existences endowed with an even intenser reality. Hence we must be on our guard that we do not allow our judgment to be warped by this unremitting pressure on our notice of the things that may be handled and seen.

There is another cause which has made materialism a favourite theory, and that is the marvellous triumphs of physical science. As it has enlarged the area of its investigations and won fresh territory from the unknown, as it has achieved a series of conquests of the most brilliant kind, it is not unnatural that its ardent votaries should forget its inherent limitations. Hence has arisen the remarkable self-confidence with which some scientists have imagined that they had in their hands the key to all knowledge. Since matter and energy seemed able to accomplish so much, we ought not to be surprised that they were hailed as competent to explain all the mysteries of the universe. And so we had Professor Tyndall, in his famous Belfast address, making the often-quoted assertion : " By an intellectual necessity I cross the boundary of the experimental evidence, and discern in that matter which we, in our ignorance of its latent powers, and notwithstanding our professed reverence for its Creator, have hitherto covered with opprobrium, the promise and potency of all terrestrial life." In spite, however, of the attractiveness which materialism possesses for the scientist, it is not likely that it will permanently maintain its ground. Some, no doubt, accept it and cleave to it, but it is more likely to be a temporary stage of thought among those who are really concerned to think out the questions that are involved. It is, indeed, a remarkable fact that some of the most eminent scientists who have at one period of their career accepted some form of materialism have been forced from it by deeper reflection. This is true of a psychologist so eminent as Wundt and a scientist so distinguished as Virchow. Those who in their eager youth were fascinated by these principles, as they came to understand more accurately the conditions of the problem, saw that materialism was inadequate to account for them.

One of the most eminent of German physiologists was Du Bois-Raymond. He had a strong inclination to materialism, and referred contemptuously to " theological madness." Yet in the very address in which this expression occurred he propounded seven problems which at the time seemed to him to be insoluble, though he anticipated that four of these might ultimately be explained. Naturally this conviction exposed him to fanatical denunciation from thoroughgoing materialists as one of the black gang, and it was a confession, all the more striking that it was extorted from him, of the intellectual bankruptcy of dogmatic materialism. The seven riddles of the universe enumerated by Du Bois-Raymond were as follows : The existence of matter and force; the origin of motion; the origin of life; the appearance of design in Nature; the existence of consciousness; intelligent thought and the origin of speech; the question of free-will. For an admirable account of this author's lecture and the controversy to which it gave rise I may refer to the Rev. J. H. Kennedy's *Natural Theology and Modern Thought*, a book which may be warmly recommended for much excellent and valuable discussion of these themes. Our present discussion is directly concerned with several of these enigmas, and recent investigations have not by any means made the problem more easy for the materialist.

I begin with the question as to the constitution of matter. It is a remarkable thing that here we are in a state of great ignorance. Matter seems to us one of the most familiar of all things, and it is precisely the scientist who has forced upon us our ignorance of its ultimate structure. Not so long ago it was the atoms which seemed to mark the final limit to which the analysis of matter could go. These atoms were, as every one knows, almost inconceivably minute. But we have passed far beyond that stage, and it is now held that the atom is itself a very complex body resembling the solar system in miniature, and consisting of corpuscles to which the name of electrons has been given. What these corpuscles are we do not know; some consider them to be electric charges, hence the name electron has been chosen to designate

them. Matter has been explained as a strain or knot
in the ether, but what ether is remains unknown, and,
even if its constitution were to be satisfactorily defined, we should only have pushed our problem a step
further back to explain and account for the elements
of which it is composed. As Mr. Whetham says in his
work, *The Recent Development of Physical Science*,
at the end of his chapter on " Atoms and Ether " :
" The ultimate explanation of the simplest fact remains, apparently for ever, unattainable." It is well
to bring out forcibly this fact that the materialist
finds his explanation of the universe in something
which is at present itself inexplicable. This is no cavil
of theologians ; it is the last word of physical science.
Moreover, how are we to account for the energy in the
universe ? The energy required for the work that
goes on even in our own small planet is tremendous
in amount, and it baffles all thought when we take
into account all the worlds of space. Is force a
property of matter, or is it something that exists
alongside of it, or is matter, perhaps, only a form of
force ? It is easy enough to build up glib theories
by conjuring with matter and motion, and we have
a right to ask the materialist what account he can
give of those factors to which everything in his system
is reduced.

I pass on, however, to other difficulties which are,
perhaps, even more cogent. In the first place, it is
opposed to the doctrine of the conservation of energy.

It is quite true, as Sir Oliver Lodge has reminded us, that possibly unknown forms of energy exist, and the theory might have to be modified if these were discovered. Still, we may take it as at present holding the field, and as, for our purpose, true. Now it has often been pointed out that we cannot account for the production of thought on materialistic principles if the law of the conservation of energy is true. This law assures us that the total stock of energy in the physical universe remains the same. For if, as a materialist has told us, the brain secretes thought, this physical process ought to involve a transformation of energy into thought, and the consequent reduction of the quantity of other forms of energy. But the truth is that the energy remains the same, and the thought thus produced is an additional product. This means that new creations are going on all the time. But these cannot be the creations of new physical energy, inasmuch as that would conflict with the law of the conservation of energy. It may be worth while to give here a quotation from Du Bois-Raymond : " The sum total of energy remains constantly the same. More or less than is determined by this law cannot happen in the material universe ; the mechanical cause expends itself entirely in mechanical operations. Thus the intellectual occurrences which accompany the material occurrences in the brain are without an adequate cause as contemplated by our understanding."

But not only does the derivation of thought from a material source contradict the doctrine of the conservation of energy, but it is a process in itself unthinkable. If it is difficult to refute the statement that "thought stands in the same relation to the brain as the gall to the liver," it is difficult simply because the proposition is absurd. It is not possible to conceive the transition from matter to thought. To say that the brain secretes thought is not profound or even clever ; it is just unmeaning, as any one who really thinks can readily see for himself. That any arrangement or rearrangement of particles of matter, even sentient and highly organised matter like the brain, could produce thought is not merely a pure fancy, and wildly fantastic at that, but utterly inconceivable.

This is freely confessed by some of the ablest scientists who have written upon the subject. For example, Professor Clifford says : "The two things are on two utterly different platforms ; the physical facts go along by themselves, and the mental facts go along by themselves." How can we imagine that the mere motions of particles of matter, even matter so endowed with sensitiveness as the brain, could produce thought ? The two things are entirely incommeasurable ; there is no common factor to bind them together.

It is also impossible to account, on materialistic principles, for even the most rudimentary form of consciousness. Kant truly said that materialism was

E

shattered on the humblest worm. The imagination is utterly baffled at the task of explaining how the chasm is to be spanned which lies between dead matter and living consciousness. It is well known that, confronted by this difficulty, some have modified materialism in such a way as to endow all matter, even the very atoms, with intellectual and emotional as well as with physical characteristics. We are familiar with the theory that matter and mind are only the same thing with two faces; and Haeckel's conjectures as to atoms with souls are put forward as the last word of science. When we read that matter and ether " are endowed with sensation and will," that they " experience an inclination for condensation, a dislike of strain; they strive after the one and struggle against the other," we are not surprised that Sir Oliver Lodge should say, " My desire is to criticise politely, and hence I refrain from criticising this sentence as a physicist should." It is quite easy to get emotion and intellect out of atoms if we have begun by putting them in; but to degrade the sacred name of science to cover grotesque metaphysics of this order is not simply culpable distortion of the facts, but it gives to matter a new and wholly illegitimate meaning. Another objection is that materialism cannot account for our conviction of personal identity. The matter of our bodies is in constant flux. Physically speaking, we are not the same thing from one moment to another. Within a certain period it may well happen that there is not a single particle in our body which was there when the period began. We ought, then, if materialism were true, to be entirely different personalities from what we were previously. But if there is one thing of which we are all convinced it is our personal identity through all physical change. We accept responsibility for the acts of the man who bore our name ten years ago, and no one would think of urging that the physical transformation that had occurred in the interval snapped the tie which bound the present to the past.

But there is a difficulty more fundamental than any other. Not only are we ignorant of what matter is, but we do not even know that matter exists at all. No doubt in our ordinary life we act on the belief that there is such a thing as an external world, and especially that matter exists in the form of our own bodies. But the only thing that we know with the absolute certainty of immediate knowledge is our own existence, and our existence not primarily on the physical, but on the mental side. All of which we are immediately aware is a stream of sensations within our consciousness. The mind sets to work on these sensations, sorts and classifies them, and draws conclusions from them. The existence of matter is not, that is to say, a fact of immediate consciousness, although to the unreflective instinct of the plain man it may seem to be so; it is an inference from the sense-perceptions.

It is quite conceivable that our physical existence and our physical environment may be an illusion, a dream from which we shall one day awake. But though every thought we have be false, a thinking mind is necessary to think them; and if our belief in a physical universe be but a dream, there must be a mind to dream it. A wild imagination, it may be said, that matter is an illusion. Yes, but not half so wild or incredible as the belief that nothing exists but matter. For we know nothing of matter except through mind. As the varied phenomena of the universe press in upon us, and pass through the organs of sense to the brain, it is the mind which uses the brain as its instrument, which understands their meaning and unifies them into a coherent whole.

Were it not for the mind the sensations which beat upon the shore of consciousness would be a wild and tumultuous crowd without meaning or coherence. It is the mind that out of these innumerable experiences extracts a meaning and builds them up into a definite and connected system. Perhaps many of my readers have had the thought which I sometimes used to have as a child, that the whole of my life was a dream and that I might any moment wake to reality. This may be improbable in the highest degree, but, after all, it is not inconceivable in the abstract. But what would be inconceivable would be that there should be a dream in which the unreal world seemed real unless there was a mind to dream it. There can be no illusion unless there is a mind to be the victim of it. Professor Huxley, after quoting Berkeley's argument that matter and motion are known to us only as forms of consciousness, and that the existence of a state of consciousness apart from a thinking mind is a contradiction in terms, proceeds : " I conceive that this reasoning is irrefragable. And, therefore, if I were obliged to choose between absolute materialism and idealism, I should feel compelled to accept the latter alternative."

I do not here press the argument from results, since I think that if a theory is true we ought to accept it, be the results what they may. Still, it is legitimate to point out that, if materialism is true, there is an end to religion and morality in any real sense of the term. But I have already tried to point out that religion is likely to be a permanent possession of the human race ; and if that position is sound, the incompatibility of religion and materialism constitutes for us a further proof that materialism is false.

It has often been urged against religion that it has led men to follow strange fancies and degrade themselves by grovelling superstition. Too often the charge has not been without its justification, but the history of materialism—especially in some of its later developments—proves that fanatical attachment to obsolete superstition is not the monopoly of religious people. And over against this materialism, which lays on matter a task it can never achieve, I confidently set the spiritual and theistic view of the universe. It would ill become a believer in God to speak with contempt of the material world, which bears the marks of His handiwork, and is the stage appointed by Him for our training. Yet the supreme thing in the universe is not matter, but spirit, and it is for the sake of spirit that matter ultimately exists. It is no far-away God in whom the Christian believes, who created the universe as a machine, and started it on its independent way. He is rather the infinite and eternal Spirit, present and active in every part of His vast creation, the strong Power in whose arms it rests, the vital energy that quickens its every movement. He is the all-wise controller of its destinies, who weaves into His great harmonious purpose all the tangled threads of its clashing impulses. He is the Infinite Being who transcends the limits of time and space. And yet in Him the deepest religious instincts are satisfied, for we are the children on whom He lavishes His love, made in His image to be His intimate companions for evermore. Into the validity of this belief it will be our next task to inquire.

CHAPTER IV

IS THERE A GOD ?

WE may take it as made good by our earlier discussion that man has everywhere developed a religion. But this very fact forces upon us the probability that Religion is not an illusion. We have been taught to recognise the importance played in development by environment. Life is one long process of interaction between organism and environment. If, then, we find everywhere in human history the presence of religion, the meaning of this fact is that there must be a spiritual universe. To deny its existence is to except religion from the great law of correspondence to environment by denying that the environment really exists. Moreover, when we remember that religion has played perhaps the most important part in human development we are confronted with this problem : How are we to understand that a faculty of such potent and far-reaching influence should have continued to exist in the absence of such a spiritual universe ? Finding no response, would it not have quickly ceased to exist ?

This consideration is powerfully reinforced by another, which is, that, in view of the rationality which is man's outstanding distinction, what has proved one of the main forces in his history should have rested upon an illusion. The precise forms which religion has assumed are comparatively unimportant for our question. The crucial point is that they all imply the existence of unknown powers with whom man may have relations. That he should have wrongly conceived the character of these powers is unimportant, for that is a mere matter of interpretation. What is vital is that there was a fact to be interpreted, not that he put this or that construction upon it. Why should the very constitution of his nature drive him thus outside himself to seek relations with higher powers if these higher powers were an empty figment? But if the source from which man drew his being planted deep within him his longing for the Eternal and the Unseen, then this stupendous fact receives an adequate explanation. Deny the existence of the Unseen Powers, and the most conspicuous feature in the history of mankind becomes an insoluble mystery.

So far what I have said does not bring us to the existence of God, but simply to the assertion that there is a spiritual universe with which man may come into fellowship. It would harmonise with the existence of many gods as well as with the existence of one. But the modern world in general has agreed that of the two alternatives we must accept a belief in one God and not in many. It is true that some recent philosophers have argued for pluralism rather than for unity on the ground that it is much easier thus to account for the existence of evil and pain without reflecting on the goodness and the love of God. I do not linger on this, however, since the difficulties with which it is encumbered seem to outweigh the advantages that it offers. The question, therefore, for us is whether there is a God or not.

I need not dwell on its importance. It is clear to all that on this our Christianity depends for its very life, and any one who knows what Christianity has been in the life of the individual and of the race will confess how great its importance is. It might have been thought that in a matter so vital if there were a God He could not have left us in such uncertainty that arguments for His existence would be required. But uncertainty is necessary to the being of faith, for if there were no uncertainty, faith would give place to knowledge. And after all our argument we do not reach demonstration, but only a high degree of probability ; so that belief in the existence of God remains to the last an act of faith. It is well to make this clear at the outset, since some might expect that the proofs should be as cogent as those used in mathematical demonstration.

There are several lines of argument by which philosophers and theologians have sought to establish the existence of God. Several of these so-called proofs have lost the force that they once seemed to possess, and they are rather too intricate and difficult to be fitly dealt with in such a volume as this. For example, when we consider the world around us, we are struck by the fact that all the phenomena we see are the effects of some cause or causes. But these causes are themselves the effects of previous causes, and so we can carry back the series of causes into the far distant past. Such is the world as we know it, and within it we cannot escape from this chain of cause and effect. But we cannot well conceive that this series should stretch back for ever. It is a logical necessity by which we think of a First Cause—a cause, therefore, not itself the effect of a preceding cause. But though I believe this argument to be valid, I do not lay stress on it here, because abstruse questions are raised as to the idea of causality, on which it would be profitless to enter; and because, while it yields to us a First Cause, it has nothing to tell us of its character. And theism, as we understand it, has very definite statements to make on this point. Nor can it be denied that we find the conception of an unoriginated First Cause very difficult to grasp.

Undoubtedly the argument from design, as it is commonly called, is the one most fitted to impress and convince the average mind. We see everywhere in Nature contrivances, adjustments, adaptations which seem to be the outcome of deliberate design.

No one who has ever considered his own body can fail to be filled with wonder at the marvels of it. If we think of the structure of the ear or the eye, even apart from any special investigation, we cannot but be astonished at it. But our astonishment passes into something like awe when we change our vague impression into exact knowledge. Think of the eye with its gift of adjustment for near or distant view, or for greater or less degree of light, and especially of the structure of the retina, on which we receive the impression of all the objects in our field of view. The retina, though of great thinness, in the ninth of its ten layers contains more than three million cones and thirty million rods. Now, we often see quoted Helmholtz's criticisms on the eye considered as an optical instrument, but it is frequently forgotten that Helmholtz went on to say that for practical purposes the eye was all the better for these theoretical imperfections. The ear consists of numerous parts, one of which, the cochlea, contains four thousand arches. Yet these structures, so complex and so minute, need for their proper working that they should be adjusted to the luminiferous ether and the waves of air, that one may paint a true picture on the retina, and the other rightly convey the sounds to the organ of hearing. Thus it is not the mere internal adjustment of the parts to each other, but of the organ itself to the medium by which the impressions are conveyed. So exquisitely fitted is the ear for its function that it

picks out the many sounds which continually strike
upon it with ease and certainty, although these sounds
are brought to it by innumerable air waves, clashing
with each other in what might seem inextricable confusion. Yet with such precision does it discriminate,
that a mistake in the interpretation of a sound is very
rare. But there is a further adjustment which must
be taken into account. In many cases we have a
striking indication of adjustment, not merely in the
medium through which the impression comes, but in
the originating cause. Thus how exquisitely the
human voice is adapted to the human ear. Were it
not for this adjustment language would be impossible.
So fine is the sense of hearing that we not only interpret the words uttered, but can differentiate between
the same words as spoken by different people ; to such
a degree of accuracy, indeed, that we can often identify
people by this sense alone, knowing them, as we say,
by their voice. But there is a still further adjustment
which has not yet been touched upon, but is, in a
sense, the most wonderful of all. It is that by which
the brain receives intelligence of and interprets the
impressions made on the organs of sense. So infallibly do the instruments set apart for this purpose
do their work, that every sight or sound registered
on eye or ear is instantaneously transmitted to the
brain, and through it is taken up into our consciousness. And the brain is so fitted for its work that,
though it receives innumerable impressions at every

moment, impressions of sight and sound and touch, it is not confused by them, but, without hesitation or delay, interprets each aright and acts accordingly. And all this is but a small part of the evidences of design furnished by a single human body. But even if we were to examine exhaustively the whole body, we should but have touched a fringe of the argument derived from the survey of the whole universe as we see it before us.

These adjustments seem to speak of purpose on a scale so vast, and betokening an intelligence so profound, as to suggest very strongly that they are due to a personal Creator of the wisest wisdom. And when our view is widened to take in not simply our own tiny planet, but all the vast worlds of space, the impression not only of intelligence, but of stupendous power, becomes almost irresistible.

It is well known, however, that it is precisely this very impressive argument from design which has been thought to be most severely hit by modern science. And before approaching this there is another objection of a general character that must not be lost sight of. The adjustment in certain cases seems to suggest a malevolent rather than a beneficent design. When the sporting man praised the creative wisdom which had tilted the nostrils of the bulldog at such an angle that he could hold on to the bull and still breathe without inconvenience, it is plain that had the bull been capable of giving his opinion he would have found it difficult to see in the arrangement the evidence of benevolent design. It is, of course, one of the difficulties under which the old-fashioned doctrine of special creation labours, that there are many things in Nature which it is hard to regard as deliberately created, and there are some adjustments which we should not have expected from a benevolent designer. It is worth while pointing out at this stage that theism is in no way committed to the theory of special creation.

The old theory of special creation, apart from other weaknesses, had this, which from a theological point of view was a salient defect—that it involved a half Deistic conception of the relation of God to Nature. The Divine activity was confined to these creative moments, and thus always assumed the appearance of an interference with the normal course of things. But, as has been well pointed out, occasional presence implies habitual absence, and the absenteeism of the Creator from His creation was a real weakness in the theory. The most religious, not to say scriptural, attitude is surely that which postulates the abiding presence and activity of God within His own universe. From that point of view the mode of creation adopted would be decided by its harmony with the character of God and His methods of working so far as we are able to discern them. And which hypothesis seems to reason—which is a God-given faculty—the most fit it is scarcely necessary to say.

The Darwinian theory of Natural Selection is often said to have discredited the argument from design. For the sake of those who may not be familiar with the theory I will give a brief sketch of it. Nature is far more prolific in the production of lives than of food to support them. Hence, as there is not enough for all, the strong survive, while the weak go to the wall. In this struggle for existence the fittest survive and the unfit are eliminated. The course of development has been largely governed by this principle of the survival of the fittest in the struggle for existence. What constitutes fitness is often some slight variation which gives a particular organism an advantage over others of its kind. It may consist in greater fleetness, by which it can better secure its prey or outdistance its pursuers ; or it may be some difference in tint, by which it approximates more closely to its surroundings, and thus more successfully eludes the notice of its enemies. But, whatever it be, the variation gives an advantage in the struggle, and the organism hands it on to its descendants, which, in course of time, since they are the fittest, alone survive, the less favoured members of the class being eliminated as unfit. Now, the bearing of this theory on the argument from design is as follows : That argument points to exquisite adaptations as given to the organism to enable it to live its life in harmony with its environment. The theory of natural selection, on the other hand, says : The organism survives in the struggle because it happens to possess some feature which gives it the advantage over other members of its class which do not possess it, and its possession is due to a fortunate variation from the common condition. Only those that thus correspond more and more closely to their environment ultimately survive ; so that at last, by successive approximations and weeding out of the unfit, the existing organism is endowed with a large number of features fitted to the environment in which it lives. In this case it would seem, at first sight, as though no directive purpose could be discerned in the adaptations. It is a matter of accident whether the lucky variation is produced at all, and, when produced, it is the competitive process that favours its preservation, not intelligent design. The argument from design, in other words, said : These adaptations are due to the action of intelligence, which thus fitted the organism to respond to its environment. The theory of Natural Selection, on the contrary, replies that the possession of these qualities which were better adapted to the environment secured the triumph of the lucky possessor ; and since all the organisms of the same species that did not possess them were ultimately killed off in the course of the struggle, the qualities themselves survived.

When Darwin first promulgated the theory it was widely felt on both sides that, if true, it demolished the argument from design. Many theologians accordingly denied that it was true, while many followers of Darwin asserted that the chief theistic proof had received its death-blow. We are somewhat wiser now. It does not fall within my plan to discuss the truth or falsity of the development theory in general, or Darwinism in particular. It seems to me, looking at the matter as a layman, that it is true, and that Natural Selection has been a real force. In any case, I am content to argue on that assumption. But we must observe the limitations of Natural Selection. In the first place, it cannot produce favourable variations. It can only preserve them when they are produced. Till variations are produced, Nature has no reason for selecting one more than another to survive ; and the development advances only when some advantageous variation makes its appearance. How, then, are we to account for the favourable variations ? It may be said that out of the abundance which Nature produces, variations from type will constantly occur. Some of these will be of no advantage to the organism, others will even handicap it in its struggle. These will perish, but other variations will be of profit, and Nature will secure their survival. Nature makes a thousand shots ; it will go hard if out of these there be not some lucky hits.

Another limitation is that Natural Selection can only preserve variations that happen to be immediately favourable. It is not variations which will be useful to the organism long afterwards, but those that serve it best in the actual conflict in which it

F

is engaged. But the very course that development has taken requires that variations should have been preserved which would be of use only in the far-distant future. And analogous to this is the further consideration that in some cases, in order to secure a certain result highly favourable to an organism, a long series of variations has had to be produced, many of which gave no immediate advantage, but were favourable only as conducting to a distant goal. In other words, purpose and prophetic foresight seem to be implied in the course which development has here taken—banking the successive variations till the time when they could be of service.

I do not dwell on the inability of Natural Selection to account for the beauty and sublimity of the universe, where no advantage in the struggle is given to these qualities. Moreover, we have to remember that, while some theory of evolution is probably correct, the newer evolutionists have moved very far from some of Darwin's most characteristic positions. Much more importance is now assigned to the inner property of change, and even sudden change, possessed by organisms. It is also now held that the struggle for existence, so far from being the main condition of development, is in itself a factor hostile and not friendly to survival. It is further held that evolution, so far from being a mechanical process, is due to a tendency to progress which resides in the organism itself. It is clear that these changes in the theory considerably modify the whole situation. It would, no doubt, be premature, while the theory is in such flux, to say precisely how we are ultimately to adjust our ideas to it. It is, however, clear already that the old view that the argument from design has been killed by Darwinism can be no longer put forward with any confidence.

Finally, I notice one highly important consideration. It is that the process of evolution has been consistently higher, moving from the lowest and simplest forms to the highly differentiated and complex, and finding its climax in man. Now, Professor Huxley was obviously right in saying that there is no reason in the nature of things why evolution should mean development upward rather than degradation. Nor, it might be added, why it should move consistently in any given direction at all. But since it has consistently meant progress, and progress culminating in such a goal, we naturally ask how is this to be explained. Let it be observed that here the question is not of the evolution of a single type, but of the universal movement. For such steady advance toward a goal demands an adequate explanation. Can we consider the method of Natural Selection taken by itself such an explanation? Observe how it works blindly, dependent on the chance of favourable variations. Yet the actual development shows us not blind movement, but progress to a definite end, in which many steps had to be taken that conferred no advantage in the struggle, while other paths which ultimately led nowhere were neglected. In other words, so far from the elimination of purpose from Nature by the method of selection, the whole process is only to be rationally interpreted as due to purpose. It is only when we put intelligence, working consciously towards a given end, into the process of Natural Selection and Evolution generally, that we have an explanation which covers the facts to be explained. Thus the argument from design, while modified by Darwinism, is really immeasurably strengthened by it, for we discover purpose now, not merely in individual adjustments, but in the whole cosmic process. The old argument from design could hardly see the wood for the trees ; the new argument takes a vaster sweep and emphasises the whole evolutionary movement as exhibiting conscious design.

I pass on to refer to the veto of agnosticism. By this is meant the view that it is impossible to affirm anything with reference to the existence of a God or a future life, since these things lie, and must lie, beyond our knowledge in the sphere of the Unknowable. It will be allowed that of this position Mr. Herbert Spencer was the most distinguished and authoritative exponent. Although he regarded the Power that works in the Universe as Unknowable, he contrived to tell us a great deal about it. He spoke of it as " an inscrutable existence, everywhere manifested, to which

we can neither find nor conceive beginning or end,"
as "an Infinite and Eternal Energy from which all
things proceed." He described it as a force analogous
to our own will, infinite, eternal, omnipresent. He
says that it "stands towards our general conception
of things, substantially as does the Creative Power
asserted by theology." But he goes even further,
and tells us that since the energy which works in the
Universe wells up in the form of consciousness in ourselves, this gives a spiritual rather than a material
aspect to the Universe. With all this it is not sur-
prising that John Fiske, a distinguished disciple of
Spencer, definitely advanced to the theistic position.
For with all these admissions Mr. Spencer himself was
not far from the kingdom of God. He halted, however,
at the crucial point, the attribution of personality to
this Eternal Energy. He did not deny it; his doctrine was not "anything more than silent with respect
to personality." But while he left it in suspense, he
insisted that if personality were not affirmed of it, we
must affirm something higher and not something lower
than personality. We need have no quarrel with that
if, at any rate, this "something higher" include
self-consciousness.

The great objection which is urged against the doctrine of a personal God is that personality implies
limitation. To this Lotze seems to have given the
true answer. We argue that personality implies
limitation, because we argue from personality as we

possess it. But really the limitation, of which we are conscious, is not due to the fact that we possess personality, but that we possess it so imperfectly. It is only the Absolute who possesses perfect personality. The Eternal Energy, Mr. Spencer tells us, wells up within us in the form of consciousness. But how thin at any given moment is the stream of consciousness! If we analyse its contents, how little they seem!

It is only a small part of our actual mental possession of which at any given moment we are aware. In the field of consciousness itself there is the focal point on which our attention is acutely centred. Shading off from that we have objects within the field of consciousness of which we are, as a matter of fact, aware, but to which our attention is only slightly directed. There are other things which are just in the margin of consciousness, but to which we are not conscious of paying any regard. But when all these things are put together, how small they are compared with the vast mass of our experience and knowledge that does not present itself to us as an object of consciousness at all. Buried below the surface in the dim recesses of the mind is all that we have ever learnt, or seen, or heard, all the experiences through which we have passed, much that we have not thought of for many years, and perhaps may never think of in this world, but still there, ready to be called up into consciousness by something that recalls it to our memory, or brought above the threshold by driving a shaft into it through such methods as crystal-gazing or hypnotism. We are only beginning to apprehend how important for each of us may be this life that goes on in the subterranean regions of our personality. How large a part it plays in our actual life is clearly seen in our automatic actions. There are many things we can do well till we think of them. As soon as we begin to reflect how we are doing them, we bungle them; they must be done automatically or there is likely to be a slip. The accomplished pianist does not think about the notes he is to strike, his fingers will go perfectly so long as they are left to themselves. I had no idea how I washed my hands till I had an attack of rheumatism, which forced the action out of the sub-conscious into the conscious domain. My hands knew perfectly well how they washed themselves. It is easy to see what a merciful provision this is which saves our feeble consciousness from being burdened with the load of so much in life. Had we to think of every step we took, how we were to take it ; of every bit of food we put into our mouths, exactly how we were to put it there ; of every word we read, how it was spelt and identified ; and of every other action that we now perform automatically, how we ought to do it, our mind would be crowded to distraction with these competing elements, reason would snap under the intolerable strain, and the world would soon be turned into a raving Bedlam. How much we have still to learn about this sub-conscious life, of the processes that go on within it, its influence on our character and conduct, the link it may form for us with other persons and with God we, as yet, scarcely dream.

While, then, we have a firm hold of personality, we have only imperfect possession of it. But we can conceive of a personality in which there should be no region of the sub-conscious or unconscious at all, where past and present and future states of consciousness were all one, and all the elements of consciousness were kept under strict control and were at the complete command of the person. Such would be perfect personality, and it would not be marked by limitation, but most conspicuously by its absence. Would not such personality be worthy of the " Infinite and Eternal Energy from which all things proceed " ? A Force analogous to our own will, which wells up in us in the form of consciousness, cannot easily be conceived as itself without self-consciousness. But, further, Mr. Spencer gives us warrant for believing that the Power which works in the Universe works for moral ends. For when he comes to construct his ethical system, on the basis of the theory of evolution, he presents us with a morality which closely resembles the ethics of Christianity. So that we may claim him as substantiating much of the theistic position, though not so fully as we could have wished. What is remarkable is that he has reached such positive results from the agnostic starting-point.

We are not, however, at the end of our quest when we have reached the result that the Universe has a Creator, or perhaps only a manipulator of matter, a Designer of supreme intelligence and power. For we cannot rest content with a Being who is merely infinite Wisdom and Power as the object of our supreme devotion and worship. We ask that He shall be endowed with Holiness and Love before we can regard Him as fit to be worshipped by us as God. And, so far, the argument has yielded to us no moral attributes at all. Are we, then, to say that the contemplation of Nature reveals to us a moral order? In other words, Is Nature on the side of virtue and against vice? Although I think, on the whole, the affirmative is probable, the view that Nature is morally indifferent is capable of defence. Indeed, we might say that Nature speaks with an ambiguous voice. Against the beneficent minister to our wants and the bountiful giver of happiness we have to set Nature the cruel, "red in tooth and claw."

If we turn from Nature to history, we find the evidence of moral character of which we are in search. Often it would seem that wickedness triumphed and that virtue went to the wall, but in the long run it would not be so. Working slowly and on a large scale we find indications of what Matthew Arnold called a Power not ourselves that made for righteousness. We see the gradual amelioration of cruelty and ferocity, the emergence and triumph of loftier ideals.

We look back over the past and see great empires rising, reigning, and then passing away. Assyria and Babylon, Persia and Rome, all of them supreme powers of the world, fell with utter ruin. And why did they fall? Because their conquests had within them the seed of their downfall. These empires were founded on bloodshed; they had the haughtiness and pride that lead to destruction, or the luxury and vice that sap the moral stamina of a nation's life. But why should these qualities bear upon them the stamp of death? Because the Power which works in history has set its face against them and works for righteousness.

It is in man, however, that the clearest proof of ethical theism is to be sought. We have within us a witness for God. I have already urged that the universal presence of religion in humanity means that religion is part of the very constitution of man. It is primary and fundamental, for were it a mere accident it could not have survived in so many races through so many ages, under such different skies, the common possession of men of character and temperament so diverse. And I have argued that we must throw the stress on the primal instinct, not on the crude, or grotesque, or even horrible forms in which it has found expression. And what does this desire for fellowship, this thirst for a living God, which is rooted in the human breast, mean but this, that the Power which has fashioned us has woven it into the very web of our being?

But while religion points to a personal God, the same testimony is borne by conscience. We have within us a sense of right and wrong, an imperative conviction of duty, which clashes sometimes with our interests, often with our pleasures, and yet which must be obeyed on the penalty of acute dissatisfaction with ourselves, and remorse for our actions. How are we to explain the presence of this strange and often unwelcome guest, withholding us from gratifications we are tempted to desire and spurring us to uncongenial deeds of goodness? Whence came that inward judge which sits to try our actions and pronounces its verdict upon them? Who gave it its regal authority? Neither Nature nor man could have produced it. This sense of right and wrong, of the eternal distinction between them, the demand that we shall follow the right, however rough the way along which it leads us, and renounce the evil, however tempting the paths down which it beckons us— these are the evidences that the Power which made us is itself moral; a Power not only of supreme intelligence and might, but also of inflexible righteousness.

Yet the most serious difficulties which theism has to encounter are moral difficulties. Let it be clearly seen, however, that they in no way weaken the argument for an all-wise Creator. If this were all that we meant by God, the argument might stop at the point already reached. But we mean much more, and cry out for a God, not only as the solution of our intellectual problems, but as the satisfaction of our hearts. And against the belief in the moral character of God weighty objections have been brought. At present I can deal with them only from the standpoint of theism; but I may so far anticipate here as to say that I think they can be dealt with most successfully from the Christian point of view. And this applies especially to what I have to say about sin.

The existence of sin is often urged as a formidable objection to belief in a good God. If God created man, not knowing that he would sin, then He is not all-wise; but if He knew it, then He is not perfectly good. Such is the dilemma on the horns of which it is supposed that we are impaled. No doubt sin is a difficulty. But some considerations may be urged in arrest of hasty judgment. We cannot take refuge in the view that God did not foresee human sin. We must take up the position that He created man with the full consciousness that he would sin, and make the best of it. Now it is clear that if God had made men incapable of sin this difficulty would have been avoided. But it is no less clear that the price would have been too costly. For then men would have been mere machines, offering to God devotion which, as compulsory, would have been worthless to Him. If the service of their hearts was to be spontaneous, they must render it freely, and must therefore be free also to withhold it. And this was God's alternative, either to create men free or not to create them at all.

In other words, Creation involves the risk of sin, in this case we may even say the certainty of it. And if this alternative is involved in the nature of the case, we ought to be sure of our ground before we criticise God for choosing one course rather than the other. We who are in the mid-stream of human history cannot rightly decide on a question which can be solved only by one who sees it as a whole from the standpoint of eternity. All we can rightly ask is that God shall vindicate His own hatred of sin, and take measures to deal with it as effectively as may be. And when the case is thus stated, even apart from the Christian solution, we may fairly hold the objection urged against the morality of God to be at least inconclusive. Added to which, I may merely note that this is one of the points at which the theory of development is very helpful to the theistic view.

It is hardly necessary to linger over the view that physical death is inconsistent with Divine goodness. Were it not for the blessed and beneficent ministry of Death the world would soon be so crowded that new births would be impossible. Life would stagnate and lose its interest, and all progress be crushed beneath the dead weight of conservatism. So far as there is anything terrible about death, it is due to sin ; and if the previous objection be disallowed, this really falls with it.

But a far more serious difficulty, as it seems to me, is that caused by pain. This, again, is mitigated by several considerations. It is probable that the pain of animals is very greatly exaggerated. They are at least spared the agonising apprehensions which often torture us much more than the actual pain itself. And we have reason to believe that they feel far less than we, in our imaginative sympathy, are apt to believe. It is not slaughter of the weak by the strong for food that constitutes the difficulty. That is, on the whole, a merciful provision of Nature, unattended with serious pain. But there are darker features which must not be ignored in the tragic story, and which we must leave as incompletely solved mysteries. If we turn to human pain, we can see that it has its function to fulfil. It preserves life by calling attention to points of danger ; and, so far as it visits us with retribution for violated law, we have no right to complain. It serves also as moral discipline, a fact attested by much experience. It is of peculiar value in that it invokes the sympathy of others, and is indeed doubly blessed in the increased refinement and tenderness of the sympathetic, and the comfort the sympathy brings to the sufferer. But when all this has been said, serious difficulties remain. I have no doubt that many feel, as I feel myself, that the most urgent argument against theism is supplied by the deliberate cruelties with the records of which history abounds. It is the torture chambers of the Inquisition, or the Armenian massacres, which furnish the most telling arguments against the goodness of God.

True, man inflicts the torture ; but, we ask, why does God permit it ? Why has He not long ago sent the Sultan of Turkey to a congenial hell ? I do not make light of these objections ; they are real and pressing. But something may be said to help us from the Christian standpoint. Meanwhile let us remember that, however great the difficulties may be, we must balance them against the group on the other side ; and also that we cannot reasonably expect to explain everything, but must leave some place for mystery. Otherwise the trial of our faith would be no trial at all. I conclude by affirming my own conviction, that the rival theories are weighted with more serious difficulties than theism ; and that the objections which may be urged against it are not sufficient to override the arguments in its favour.

CHAPTER V

WHICH IS THE BEST RELIGION?

SINCE we have reached the conclusion that man must have a religion, the question now arises, which of the competing religions best satisfies our ideal of what a religion should be? At this stage of our inquiry no question is raised as to the truth of this or any other religion. The method here adopted is that of first discovering the worthiest religion, and only then asking if it be true. We shall be best able to judge of worth if we begin by stating what tests we may expect a religion to satisfy, what tests it must satisfy, if we are to accept it. No doubt it may be urged that there is a danger lest those tests should be selected which Christianity meets most successfully, and thus an undue favouritism determine beforehand which religion shall win the crown. I hope that the tests actually chosen will justify themselves; but I may add that we are warranted in appealing to Christianity for suggestion here, since such excellences as it possesses may reasonably be required in any religion that seeks to rival it, unless, indeed, the latter has compensatory virtues in which Christianity is deficient.

The first test grows directly out of the nature of religion itself. It is, Does a given religion attempt to secure fellowship with God ? Now, this is not an element in religion suggested simply by Christianity. Communion with the higher powers is an almost constant feature in religions, which manifests itself in prayer and sacrifice. Next, Does it combine with this a worthy conception of God, and thus secure the reverence and awe for Him which alone make true worship possible ? We cannot worship a God less worthy than ourselves in our best moments ; we must feel that He is infinitely holy as well as infinitely kind. And this leads me to mention the third test, Does it recognise sin as the virulent poison that it is, reckon with and try to overcome it ? Our conscience demands this, as well as our conception of God. If He is holy, sin must hinder that communion with Him in which the essence of religion consists. Sin, as we know it in human life, is an evil that demands radical treatment, and a religion which claims to be the highest must be competent to deal with it as it deserves. Further, we are entitled to ask that it throw the weight of its influence on the side of morality. On this I need not dwell. We may also insist that it shall serve humanity and work for progress. The elevation of society and the individual are worthy aims of the highest religion ; indeed,

G

essential if it is to be the highest. Lastly, it must be a universal religion—that is, appeal to man as man, independently of any limitations of race or time, of country or nationality. It does not need to be proved that such limitations disqualify for the prize.

Now, it is quite plain that these tests exclude at once the vast number of historical religions. Three of these alone can be called universal religions— Buddhism, Islam, and Christianity — and the right of Islam to a place in this list is not uncontested. But even if it survive this test, it fails to satisfy others. It emphasises the greatness of God, but in such a one-sided way that He is regarded as far too great, and man as too abject, for fellowship to subsist between them. And out of this, too, springs its paralysing fatalism, which makes progress impossible —a defect which is patent to all who know what Mohammedan countries are. The position it accords to woman (a sure test of its social quality) is low. Its moral code is also not high. These defects are in the religion itself, not due to defective practice on the part of its adherents. Buddhism, again, is fundamentally atheistic, and therefore cannot provide fellowship with God. Attempts to supply this defect have been made, but at the price of the degradation of the religion. Buddhism is also pessimistic; and while, in one respect, this is its glory—for it was begotten of the great pity of its Founder for the woes of man—yet it is also its condemnation. For while it recognises the terrible evils of the world, it does not confront them with any hope of removing them. How could it, when it teaches that existence is itself an evil?

Of these three historic religions Christianity remains. Will it also fail to satisfy these conditions? I believe that it meets them all. It has a very lofty conception of God. It has taken up and made its own the great passages in which the prophets of Israel declared His incomparable holiness and majesty. It insisted on His spirituality, and demanded in harmony with it a worship in spirit and truth. But while the greatness of God was asserted and reverence in His worship was enjoined, these were not so emphasised as to make fellowship with God impossible for man. Jesus taught His disciples to say, " Hallowed be Thy Name," but He had first taught them to say, " Our Father." And Father on His lips was the highest name He could give. It expressed the essential kinship of man with God and the great truth that He had made us in His image, that this, indeed, constitutes us men. Since, then, all men are His offspring, there is that community of nature which makes fellowship with Him possible. But, further, Christianity teaches that in the Incarnation of the eternal Son, God has entered into the life of man and taken humanity into Himself. Thus by an act of marvellous grace and sacrifice God and man have been brought together. And this may be realised by each individual in his own experience, for by faith all may enter into personal union with Christ. Thus man rises to share in that blessed communion which subsists between the Father and the Son. And since the intrinsic worth of fellowship depends on the character of the God with whom we have communion, it may be claimed that in Christianity this is of the highest type, for it teaches that God is Love, and that He has proved it by the sacrifice of His Son. And it is unique in its success in fusing the righteousness and the love of God into a perfect unity by its doctrine of the Fatherhood of God.

Again, it recognises the fact of sin, deals with it, and overcomes it. No doubt it creates difficulties for itself by its frank admission of the fact of sin. The existence of moral evil is a stumbling-block to faith. If it could be denied or ignored, a great burden would be lifted from men's minds. It is, therefore, to the honour of Christianity that it does not attempt to palliate it, much less to ignore it. More than any other religion it emphasises its heinousness, treats it as the worst of all evils, insists on its universality, throws all its strength into the conflict with it. It is not paralysed in the face of so awful a power. It measures its full strength, is well aware how stubborn and prolonged the struggle with it will prove, yet is triumphant in the full assurance of ultimate victory. No other religion has so seriously taken in hand, as one of its main tasks, to extirpate the power of sin. It is pre-eminently a religion of redemption.

The loftiness of its morality will hardly be disputed. Not only did it inculcate those ethical laws which were generally recognised in the best ethical systems of its time, but it added new virtues, of which humility may be taken as an example. But it did more than this. It made a single principle, and that the highest— love—the root of the finest and loftiest life. And thus, by reducing all to one great principle, it freed the moral life from the tyranny of endless and perplexing questions as to the adjustment of the claims of this commandment or that. Love was made the supreme arbiter of conduct. But Christianity did even more. It exhibited the moral ideal in a Person, and thus once for all expressed the highest morality, not in a string of commandments, but in the character of a Man who had lived and died as the type of all perfection. Consider how great this is, to have delineated for us a character in which holiness is incarnate, so that henceforth when we think of the ideal we do not add virtue to virtue, but think of Jesus of Nazareth. I need not say how immeasurably greater is the power of a personal ideal than that of a set of abstract rules. And Christianity has made love to this Person the supreme virtue, in which all other virtues are potentially included. For love to Him implies a growing likeness to Him. Nay, more, it brings the Christian into vital union with Him, and thus communicates new life and new character.

Does it satisfy the last test—that is, does it serve

to elevate mankind? It teaches that God is the Father of all men, and therefore that all men are brothers. It bids us see in the most vicious and degraded, children of our common Father, whom we must love and for whose emancipation we must toil. It cannot be a matter of indifference to us that our brothers should live in privation and misery, in ignorance and vice. It is to Christianity that we owe the enthusiasm for humanity. Take the most advanced peoples at the time of Christ's birth. The Jews were the Ishmaelites of the ancient world, repaying hate and scorn with a hate and scorn still deeper. How powerful was the spirit of the new religion may be seen in the case of Paul, who was changed by it from a bigoted and fanatical Jew into the great apostle of the Gentiles, and often dwelt with wondering gratitude on the cancelling of all distinctions of race and culture and social status through the cross of Christ. The Greeks looked down on all other peoples as barbarians, and the Roman was still haughtier in his imperial pride. But there is a darker stain still. No feature in ancient society is more constant or assumes larger proportions than that of slavery. It was defended by the greatest of Greek philosophers on the theory of racial inferiority, by the Roman lawyers as a commutation for the death of the vanquished in war. Christianity taught that no such inferiority existed, that God had made all of one blood, and that all men were brothers. When Paul sent back Onesimus to Philemon, no longer a slave, but above a slave, a brother beloved, when he said that in Christ there could be neither bond nor free, he struck at the very root of slavery by enunciating the principle that no Christian could regard his brother man as a slave. But the humanitarian temper of Christianity is shown in many other ways. To it we owe the energetic provisions for the alleviation of suffering, to which the ancient world was callous, the mitigation of the horrors of war, the regard for human life, and the elevation of woman. Care for the poor has, from the very first, played a large part in the activities of the Church.

It may, of course, be said that all this quietly ignores much that may be charged against Christianity. What of the rack and the stake and all the other accursed horrors of the Inquisition, due to zeal for Christianity? What, too, of the treatment of the natives of America by the Spaniards, and of slavery in the West Indies and the Southern States? What of all the other evils perpetrated in the name of Christianity, and for which the sanction of the religion has been invoked? These are a dishonour to Christendom, but they are not to be charged to Christianity. They have no shadow of support in the teaching of Christ or the apostles. They stand, as I have already pointed out, in radical opposition to the fundamental principles of the Gospel. The old heathenism is still deeply rooted in society; only slowly can Christianity make its way. For very much that goes by the name is quite foreign, and it is not fair to confound the nominal with the real.

But it is not only by its doctrine of brotherhood that Christianity works for the elevation of mankind. It is only in it that the individual has received his true place. In antiquity the worth of the individual was greatly under-estimated; he was unduly subordinated to the community. But the Christian religion, by insisting on the infinite value of each human soul, and by asserting the greatness of its destiny, supplied an immense incentive to the attainment by each of the highest within reach. The doctrine of the worth of man is, to all who accept it, a powerful stimulus in the struggle to a fuller and deeper life. An interest in mankind in the mass is compatible with heartless indifference to the lot of individuals. But Christianity works for true progress by its recognition that every individual should be the object of its loving service, while it is not unmindful of the need for the amelioration of society.

Further, Christianity is possessed of an invincible belief that no man is to be despaired of. He may be so degraded that the last hope of reform may seem to have gone. He may be so hardened that every appeal may seem to fall blunted from his iron-bound heart. But Jesus taught His followers to despair of none, to count no man beyond reach. Thus missionaries have laboured on in patience for many years, seeing no fruit of their labour, not giving up the task, though often tempted to despair. Others have toiled among the outcast and the vicious, and though their work seemed foredoomed to failure they have been upheld by their Master's confidence that the worst may be saved. And in this Christianity exhibits its power to serve and uplift mankind. Its arm would be unnerved for its work if defeat were accepted as inevitable. But it will not abate its confidence that in every man there is a spark of good which may be quickened into a living flame.

We are surely, then, entitled to say that, better than any of the other historic religions, Christianity satisfies the tests to which any religion that claims our adhesion may legitimately be submitted. There are other competitors which might be considered. But they can hardly be thought superior, as religions, to Christianity ; and if they command acceptance, it is with those who think that the truth of the facts on which Christianity rests is insufficiently substantiated. It is not necessary to speak further of them now. Nor will it be needful to consider them if the subsequent discussion establish not simply that Christianity is the best religion, but also that it is true.

CHAPTER VI

THE TRINITY IN UNITY

THE doctrine of the Trinity is the foundation on which the stately structure of Christian theology reposes. To the man in the street this doctrine seems often to exhibit the theologian at his worst. Here we have, the plain man is inclined to say, the love of theological subtleties, the hair-splitting definition, the passion for the mysterious and incomprehensible carried to the climax of appropriate absurdity. It seems an arithmetical puzzle which shocks the reverence of the more devout, while it provokes the derision of those who pride themselves on a robust common sense.

With the scruples of reverence I have the warmest sympathy. It is true that theologians have often been tempted to push their investigations into regions where they have no right to tread, and to solve the impenetrable mysteries as if they were schoolboy problems. To pass into the Holy of Holies with bold and confident step, with no sense that we are treading on sacred ground, would be profane indeed. But it was no desire to mystify the unlettered believer, no delight in spinning theological subtleties for their own sake, no proud confidence in their own intellectual agility and power, that impelled the theologians of the Church to formulate this doctrine. We entirely misunderstand it if we look at it as a performance in speculative gymnastics, the feat of intellectual acrobats.

The doctrine was created not so much in a speculative as in a religious interest. It was no metaphysical subtlety, no unnecessary burden placed on faith by the ingenuity of theologians. Not philosophy, but the Christian revelation attested by the Christian consciousness forced the Church to construct the abstract doctrine in order that she might safeguard what was vital to her existence. And it was with some reluctance that she undertook the task, profoundly conscious, at any rate in her greatest representatives, how perilous and difficult a path she essayed. But when the great redemptive facts, apart from which she had no meaning and could maintain no permanence, were in mortal peril, what could she do but take up the gauntlet that had been flung down and develop the truths that were implicit in her belief? This is not to approve of the methods by which the truth was formulated and enforced. But we may humbly believe that through all the imperfection of human instruments which seemed, indeed, so intractable to His hand God was guiding to their right conclusion the mighty issues of the debate.

I turn, then, to consider the causes which compelled the Church to formulate this doctrine if she was to guard the truth committed to her charge. And first I must speak of its historical development. The doctrine is specifically Christian, and not Jewish. There is no doctrine of the Trinity in the Old Testament. The idea that the mystery is hinted in the use of the plural word for God, Elohim, with the singular verb, or in the thrice-repeated cry of "Holy" in the Song of the Seraphim, may be confidently set aside. It is clear, indeed, why the revelation of this doctrine would have been premature. It would probably have created a new polytheism. In a world where polytheism was rampant the first necessity was to stamp deep into the consciousness of Israel the unity of God. It has been hard enough in the Christian Church itself to keep out tendencies to polytheism, whether as survivals of the old paganism or an exaggeration of the distinctions within the Godhead into a belief in three Gods. It would have complicated the problem enormously if, when every nerve had to be strained to hold fast the unity of God, the doctrine of the Trinity had been prematurely revealed.

Yet there were tendencies in the Old Testament itself which foreshadowed the breaking up of the abstract unity in the direction subsequently taken by Christianity. The description of the Divine Wisdom, in the eighth chapter of Proverbs, as God's possession in the beginning of His ways, set up from everlasting before the foundations of the earth, His companion and master-workman in the task of creation, is a very striking anticipation of the later doctrine. So " the Presence of Yahweh " or " the angel of His presence," a conception difficult to grasp, because not quite to be identified with Yahweh, nor yet easily distinguishable from Him, is another such anticipation. Similarly, we might refer to the doctrine of the Spirit in the later chapters of Isaiah.

With the growing sense of the majesty of God, and His separation from mankind that marked the post-exilic period, there were other developments which contributed directly or indirectly to the New Testament doctrine. Intermediaries were inserted between God and the universe, both to keep the Supreme Being aloof from the trivial concerns of man, and in another form of speculation to keep Him from contact with matter. On the one side, this found expression in an elaborate doctrine of angels. On the other side, especially in the Jewish Platonism of Alexandria represented most conspicuously by Philo, it introduced into Jewish thought the doctrine of the Logos, a term which bore not simply the sense of " Word," but even more strongly the sense of " Reason."

Such, then, were the tendencies already at work in Judaism which prepared the way for the Christian doctrine. It cannot be said that they yield to us any real distinction within the Godhead. They are rather vivid personifications than distinct persons. Yet they prepared the mould into which the Christian facts might be poured, and the terminology in which the Christian doctrine could find expression. It must be remembered, however, that the doctrine of the Trinity itself came to full expression only at a comparatively late period. The Church did not start out with the doctrine of the Trinity, and seek to construct in the light of it the great facts of revelation and redemption. She started from the facts and moved forward slowly to a goal of which she was only dimly conscious for much of her way. The formulation of doctrine grew out of the historical manifestation, and, till the Son of God had been revealed, the basis for the doctrine in experience was lacking. Moreover, not only was there no formulation of the doctrine before the coming of Christ, but there is no explicit formulation of it in the New Testament itself.

There are, however, striking Trinitarian formulæ in the New Testament. First of all we have the baptismal formula : " Baptising them in the name of the Father, and of the Son, and of the Holy Ghost." I do not press this as though it were an endorsement of the ecclesiastical doctrine on the lips of Jesus Himself, since the authenticity of the saying is disputed by several critics ; but I would point out that in our earliest New Testament documents, the Pauline Epistles, formulæ of this kind occur, and, since we have no trace of controversy in the Church aroused by them, it remains a plausible explanation that Jesus

Himself had uttered the words ascribed to Him in the baptismal commission. We have especially the apostolic benediction in 2 Corinthians xiii. 14. In 1 Corinthians xii. 4–6 we have a remarkable co-ordination of the Spirit, the Lord, and God. And there are several other passages that might be quoted from the New Testament in this connexion.

The question of the divinity of Christ is so important and fundamental that I must devote a special discussion to it, and therefore do not exhibit the evidence for it here. But the early Christians held together two lines of thought which logically forced them to the ecclesiastical doctrine of the Godhead. On the one side they held fast as against polytheism the unity of God ; on the other hand they asserted the divinity of Christ. It is by no means uncommon for people to keep two apparently inconsistent ideas in their mind, unrelated and unreconciled. But, sooner or later, logic does its work and forces them either to reconcile the ideas or abandon one of them.

We learn from Tertullian that there were many Christians unversed in theology who dreaded the doctrine of distinctions within the Godhead, since they imagined that this involved a relapse into polytheism. Hence arose such expressions as " I believe in one God, Jesus Christ," or the view that Father and Son were identical. This tendency found its fullest expression in the Sabellian doctrine that Father, Son, and Spirit were but three modes or aspects under which the one God successively revealed Himself. But this did not satisfy the deeper thinkers of the Church. It led to inextricable confusion and conflicted with the phenomena of the Gospel history, which represented a marked distinction as existing between Jesus and the Father. How could it be thought that Jesus was identical with the Father to whom He prayed, or how could He utter the agonised cry, " My God, My God, why hast Thou forsaken Me? " The problem, therefore, could not be solved along such simple lines as these. It must succeed in combining the unity of God with the distinction of Father and Son, and the same applied to the Holy Spirit.

In our own time it is not uncommon to hear interpretations of the Trinity which recall to us the old Sabellianism. All the personal distinctions in the Godhead are denied, and we learn that the Father is God in Nature, the Son God in Christ, the Spirit God in History or in the Church. Such formulæ as these, while they are superficially attractive, nevertheless cut the vital meaning out of the Gospel. They are not really compatible with the doctrine of Christ's divinity as we are familiar with it in Christian theology, and they lose all that positive wealth of moral and metaphysical significance which we find in the doctrine of the Church.

A reconciliation was sought along the lines of regarding the Son and Spirit as beings of inferior essence I do not enter into the different forms which this doctrine assumed, culminating, as they did, in the various types of Arianism. Here, again, the Church felt that injustice was done to her facts. She was sure of the real and essential divinity of her Founder and Redeemer ; she offered prayer to Him and not simply in His name. Therefore she could not assign to Him the position of a creature whose co-existence with the Father was not eternal, and at the same time do justice to the Christian consciousness as to His work and the position assigned to Him in Christian devotion. The issue of the long debate was the definite formulation of the doctrine of the Trinity in Unity.

When we confess this truth we should not think of it merely as expressing the fact that God manifests Himself to us as a Trinity in creation, revelation, and redemption. We regard this manifestation as corresponding to essential and eternal distinctions within God Himself. Now it is easy to criticise this doctrine as the height of unreason. Many regard it as really denying the unity of God while formally asserting it. Nothing would be gained by so insisting on the unity as to cancel any real distinctions between the persons. Unquestionably the orthodox Christian means to affirm the unity of God as earnestly as the non-Trinitarian. He believes, in fact, that his doctrine steers the middle course between deism and pantheism. He is well aware that here the path narrows to a razor edge, for how is he to state the truth so as to avoid Sabellianism on the one hand and tritheism

H

on the other ? How secure at once the plurality and the unity ? But that seems to him no reason for impoverishing his faith by declining to accept the perilous enterprise. The great theologians have freely conceded the insufficiency of all human statement ; and we may at least be sure that a doctrine of the Godhead with the element of mystery eliminated could not in the nature of things be true.

We must remember that we cannot apply to the inner life of God considerations which are simply true of human experience. In the nature of the case the interior life of God must be largely unimaginable to us. We may expect it to exhibit a blending of characteristics which on our own lower plane of existence would be mutually exclusive. Obviously human life is no measure for the life of God, and if we set to work constructing it from the facts of our consciousness or our social relations, we shall arrive at very incomplete results. If it be true that God exists as a Trinity in Unity, we can know this only through revelation, and finite creatures are plainly no judges of what may or may not be possible in the existence of an infinite Being.

Moreover, it is very important to remember that human language is the precipitate of human experience. Hence all the terms it has at command are terms which are in a sense vitiated for its purpose by this radical limitation. For how can any terms which have been created to express human experience, and have human associations clinging about them, be adequate to set forth the inner life of the Divine, which has no analogy in human experience, and therefore no terminology in human language? Hence such terms as " person " and " substance," " subsistence " and " essence," " generation " and " procession," while they are used in the technical phraseology of the subject, have inevitably misleading suggestions associated with them. For example, the technical term for describing the subsistences that make up God is Person. Originally this meant a mask; hence the phrase, three persons, originally bore a Sabellian significance, that Father, Son, and Spirit were terms expressing three different aspects. The sense of the term has shifted, so that now three persons in common language would imply, not the same individual in three aspects, but three distinct individuals; but we cannot apply that to the doctrine of the Trinity, otherwise we fall over at once into tritheism. We may say that the truth lies between the sense of person as aspect and its sense as individual, but how we are to combine the distinction with the unity is a problem wholly beyond the wit of man, because we have no analogy in our experience to qualify us for understanding it. For us persons are mutually exclusive individuals; the persons in the Godhead are mutually inclusive: there is a mutual indwelling of each in the others.

But while it is not possible to evolve the doctrine

of the Trinity from our own inner consciousness, or adequately to express it in human language, yet once it has been revealed to us we are able to see a depth and richness of meaning in it that otherwise we might not have realised. For the doctrine of the Trinity provides us with a conception of God which answers our speculative problems and satisfies our religious needs.

In the first place, it helps to secure the Personality of God. In our own case the consciousness of personality is aroused and sustained by the sense of contrast between the self and the not-self into which we divide the universe. We distinguish ourselves from the world about us. Thus we come to apprehend our own personality, and sharply to define its limits. We may see in the distinctions within the Godhead that which makes the divine self-consciousness possible. It might be urged, however, that this could be secured by the existence of the external universe. But to that there are two objections. In the first place, it would impair the absoluteness of God, since He would depend for the realisation of His personality on something external to Himself. And the material universe would not be adequate for the purpose. We achieve a sense of our own personality only in the society of our fellows. We can win it to a certain extent by contrast with animate and inanimate nature, but the deepest elements of our personality can find their satisfaction only in those who are constituted as ourselves. And, similarly, the material universe could never suffice for the need of the Creator. But neither can we make God dependent for self-realisation on personalities outside Himself. This would mean that God could not be completely God till He had created spirits for fellowship with Himself, and so once again His absoluteness would be impaired and the Infinite made to depend on the finite for His perfection. Thus the doctrine of the Trinity guards the personality of God.

Similarly we know that for the existence of a moral life society is necessary. Here, too, the doctrine of the Trinity helps us because it ensures for us the essential morality of God. In that divine society of unity which is the home of difference moral relations have eternally existed. And, pre-eminently, this is true of love. We do not think of love as a moral attribute of God; it is the very essence of His moral being. And the doctrine of the Trinity assures us that love has not been merely a potentiality latent in God to be subsequently called into activity when He created new spirits that He might escape from solitude; but in the circle of His own being there were always the lover and the loved. Thus He did not need to go outside of Himself to find the perfection of His moral any more than of His metaphysical being. He is the self-sufficient God.

We do not speak of the lonely God as some have done, for from eternity He is the perfect society, needing for His beatitude no being outside Himself. And thus God did not need the world of created spirits to satisfy His life. Hence it was not the compulsion of an inward necessity or the thirst for His own content which impelled Him to the work of creation. When He called the universe into being there was no tinge of self-seeking in His act, but only the impulse of a boundless love to create an innumerable multitude of spirits as objects of His beneficence. Thus the doctrine of the Trinity meets the demand that the Absolute should be the home of moral and spiritual relations.

I am well aware that much which has been said seems to involve simply a duality and not a Trinity in God. The thought that the distinction of subject and object is a necessary safeguard for the personality and the love of God is satisfied by the recognition within the Godhead of Father and Son. I doubt whether the ingenious attempts that have been made to infer on speculative grounds the third centre of self-consciousness within the Godhead really carry much conviction with them. If, then, we assert that the Godhead consists not merely of Father and Son, but of Father, Son, and Spirit, we do so simply in loyalty to what we conceive to be implied in the teaching of the New Testament.

The doctrine of the Trinity, then, expresses the richness and fullness of the life of God and its sufficiency for itself. The postulates, that self-consciousness depends for its existence on a society, that the self can know itself only through contrast with the not-self, and, further, that love necessitates the lover and the loved, find their satisfaction in the Christian conception of God as no bare and abstract unity, but a unity rich and complex, embracing different centres of consciousness in mutual relation. Thus we secure the conditions both of a personal and a moral life in God without needing to call in the help of an eternal creation. That life we can only dimly hint at in vague and imperfect phrases, but even the obscure twilight in which we move need not cause us to doubt the reality of whose vast proportions we can form no conception and whose outline we only faintly discern.

CHAPTER VII

SIN

I HAVE said that it was no inward necessity to escape from solitude which constrained God to the task of creation, but the impulse of a boundless love to create spirits as objects of His beneficence. But when we contemplate the universe as we actually know it, this thought of the unselfish God, seeking to enlarge the sphere of happiness and creating those who could participate in His bliss, seems to receive a violent contradiction. For here, instead of the sweet harmony of creatures wholly attuned to the will of their Creator and finding their highest beatitude in fellowship with Him, we behold a world in arms against its Maker and see evil in all its hideous forms abounding on every hand.

It is a problem before which the greatest men have had to confess defeat when they have sought for an adequate solution of the question, "How can we account for the emergence of evil in a universe created by One who is Himself all-wise, all-powerful, and holy?" Towards the close of his great work *Microcosmus*, Lotze says: "No one has here found the thought which would save us from difficulty, and I, too, know it not." Yet we are not without some helpful suggestions which, if they still leave much margin, as we might have anticipated, for mystery, yet help to lift from us the burden of the irrational. The problem of evil is one which all philosophers have to confront, for imperfections and moral disharmony are stamped so deeply into the fabric of life that any thinker who sets himself seriously to explain the scheme of existence is forced to make room in his solution for this tragic element.

Yet sin is specifically a religious term. The moral teacher speaks of vice which corrupts the nature and defies the law of man's being. The law is familiar with crime, which violates its behests and introduces a disturbing element into civic and social life. But it is only theology that can speak of sin, that regards the disposition or conduct of the creature as involving a false and wrong attitude to God. And of all religions Christianity has taken sin with the greatest seriousness. She has not palliated it or tried to explain it away, she has insisted on its heinousness with a power that has never been equalled. Nothing can show more clearly the awful gravity with which she has thought of sin than the fact that she regards the extremest measures as necessary to overcome it. It is in no dogmatic statement as to the exceeding sinfulness of sin that its judgment is expressed, but in the fact that the death of God's own Son was conceived to be necessary to its atonement and extirpation. The Cross of Christ reveals to us what God thinks and feels about sin. This stern and austere judgment of sin is a high tribute to the lofty morality of the Gospel. For the darker the picture she draws of sin the greater the difficulty she creates for herself in maintaining her affirmation of the wisdom and purity of God.

Nothing, then, is more alien from the Christian religion than to make light of sin or to treat it in a flippant and frivolous way. We must seek to think of it as God thinks of it, and what God thinks of it we see on Calvary. We have to recognise that it is a virulent poison, utterly and irremediably bad, something not to be treated with lenient indifference, but to be pursued with alert and relentless hostility. But while this is the judgment that we pass upon sin, we must beware of morbid exaggeration on the other side. It does not follow, because sin is a rabid poison, that we must pronounce the same verdict on the sinner that we do on sin.

We must beware of the gross extravagances with which man's state has too often been depicted. These inevitably provoke a recoil, and we are suffering to-day from the effects of the lurid pictures drawn by the theologians of an earlier time. We should, for example, carefully avoid the use of such terms as " total depravity." I am well aware that this term is explained to mean simply that there is no part of a man which is untouched by evil, and as so interpreted the statement becomes quite unobjectionable. But any one who will read the language of the older divines with reference to this subject will not readily believe that this was all that they meant to assert. And it is surely not merely injudicious, but positively mischievous, to continue the use of this highly objectionable expression to cover what is little better than a mere truism. We can speak of man's total goodness with just as much right as of man's total depravity in this modern use of the phrase. In other words, there is no part of man's nature that is untouched by the power of good. But I do not hear any of the modern defenders of the one phrase suggest that we should adopt the other. Similarly the assertion that sin is an infinite evil may be so explained as to express an element of truth. But it also I take to be so misleading to the plain man, and in its obvious sense so irrational, that I should banish it altogether from the vocabulary of theology.

The difficulties which the problem presents have naturally led to several solutions. In the first place I must mention those theories according to which sin does not really exist at all. This is a characteristic feature of pantheism. It is sometimes said that pantheism makes God the author of sin. If there is nothing outside God, then the evil in the universe must belong to Him as well as the good. This criticism really does not go deep enough, for the pantheist cannot consistently admit that evil exists at all; it is only our finite point of view which lends the appearance of evil to what we call sin. Could we rise from our limited standpoint to behold the universe as it really is, we should see that evil and sin were mere illusion. This way of escape is impossible to the Christian who asserts the reality of the self and refuses to allow the individual to be lost in the whole. For him evil is real, sin is a terrible fact. And even those who do not share the Christian standpoint for the most part readily enough admit that evil cannot be explained away any more than the existence of the finite self.

Many, again, deny all reality to sin because they deny the freedom of the will. For them man is a mere machine who has no part in his own creation or in the environment into which he was plunged at his birth. Everything in him is the result of external forces, and therefore he has no real responsibility for his acts. Were this true, it would be foolish to talk about sin; the term would be meaningless. It would carry us too far to enter on the tremendous problem of free-will and determinism, but the following observations may be made. It is quite true that the extent to which the will is free has been largely over-estimated in popular belief. We are very largely determined by our ancestry and our environment. These create the conditions in which we have to play our part, they select the field on which we fight and the foes with whom we have to wrestle. But they do not do everything, there is an irreducible element of personality which is our very own.

There is no fact of experience to which the testimony of consciousness is more explicit than the fact that we possess a certain measure of choice. If it is said that the will follows the strongest motives, it must be said, on the other hand, that the will pits motives one against the other and shifts their balance. It often, in fact, converts a weak motive into a strong one, and by identifying itself with this proves the freedom with which it exerts its choice. There is no fact more certain than this—that in the moment of choice we are conscious of our freedom, we are conscious that while we select one motive we might select another, and after the act has been done we are aware that we might have acted differently.

If we are absolutely determined and the will is in no sense free, we cannot account for that feeling of remorse, to which none of us is a stranger, which tells us that we were not swept along by forces we could not control, but that in the guilty deed we identified ourselves with our act. This, be it observed, is an immediate and universal affirmation of consciousness. That there are psychological puzzles connected with it no one would deny, or that a very strong case in logic could be made out against the possibility of free-will. But these difficulties do not warrant us in rejecting that of which we are directly aware, and the reality of which is attested by the existence of remorse. It is, moreover, a significant thing that the most pronounced advocates of determinism always act as if they were free themselves, and mete out praise and blame in a way that their theory, if it were true, would render absurd.

Again, some virtually deny the real evil of sin by the assertion that sin is necessary to the artistic perfection of the universe. We must have the dark shades in our picture as well as the light. It is only through the contrast with evil that good can be known and appreciated. What seems to us disharmony when viewed in itself blends into a perfect harmony when we view the Great Whole. There is, of course, a sense in which we may speak of evil as throwing good into relief and bringing out its intrinsic excellence more sharply by contrast, but we have no right to palliate evil on this ground. Moreover, are we to carry this moral difference into the life of God Himself, and say that for His perfection and the complete harmony of His being evil is necessary to Him as well as good ?

Nor can we treat sin as something merely negative, a defect and nothing more. For many of the forms in which it manifests itself show that it is no mere negation of good, but that a positive heinousness attaches to it. The crimes which fill us with horror, the atrocities that stir us with indignation to the depths, the insolence which crushes man with cold contempt, the ambition that moves through blood to its goal and counts nothing of the hearts it has broken, and many another form of sin familiar to us all, is not something that can be described by pale negatives, but something which is actively and aggressively bad.

Nor can we rightly say that evil is a form of good. To describe it as good in the making might be plausible in a certain range of instances, but this would be quite misleading as a general definition. Nor can we speak of evil as perverted good. It has often been pointed out that what drives the sinner to his sin may sometimes be the sense of dissatisfaction which, if he only knew it, is the cry of his nature for God. And there is no doubt an element of truth in this assertion. Nevertheless, one would need to be blind to some very patent facts to regard this as accounting for more than a comparatively small proportion of sin. Christianity, moreover, will not substitute fine phrases for brutal realities, but insists on the hard fact that sin must be treated as the fundamentally evil thing that it is. A man may no doubt seek to still his vague unrest in the pleasures of the world, but sin, for the most part, is a much more commonplace thing than that ; it is a deliberate quest for self-gratification rather than the blind plunge into the Infinite, the search for a fuller and intenser life in God. I can conceive a sin prompted by desire to escape from the cramped life of the finite self to the intoxicating sense of a larger experience. But usually it is the victory of the baser over the loftier self.

We reach, then, the conclusion that sin is real, and that we can escape from our difficulty neither by denying its existence, by palliating its badness, nor by turning it into a form of good. And so we return to the problem why in a world governed by a holy, all-wise, and all-powerful God sin was permitted to emerge at all. It would be no answer to say that the very conditions of creaturely existence imply imperfection. It is obvious that they do. What has been called metaphysical evil must attach to the whole of created being. This, however, simply means that the creature must be finite, but there is no necessary connexion between limitation of being and sinfulness of character. It is not sin to fall short of a perfection which in the very nature of the case lies beyond our reach ; the sin consists in the fact that we do not rise to such perfection as lies within our grasp.

Nor is it the case that our physical conditions necessitate the sinfulness of our career. It is very natural that such a view should have arisen. It is so constantly our experience that the sensuous side of our nature betrays us into wrongdoing that we readily express the evil which besets us in the terms of a conflict between the flesh and the spirit. The higher nature we identify with our spirit, the lower with the body. Our physical passions and impulses are those which seem to us mainly responsible for our tragic

moral difficulties. Could we only get rid of this schism
in our nature, it seems as though all might be well.
We should escape from the tyranny of matter, and
the spirit would wing upwards its unimpeded flight.
Yet when we come to think of it we can hardly feel
satisfied with such an explanation. Doubtless it is
true that many forms of sin are of a physical character,
but it would be gross exaggeration to apply this explanation to all of them. There are many forms of
sin that could be practised just as well by a disembodied spirit. To feel the emotions of anger and
hatred, of envy and jealousy, of vanity and pride, a
bodily organism is not necessary. Moreover, precisely
the same physical act may be sinful or legitimate
according to circumstances. It is perfectly legitimate
and, indeed, necessary for us to eat food, but if our
food is attained by theft, the eating, otherwise legitimate, becomes sinful.

What, no doubt, has contributed to the widespread
connexion of sin with our physical nature is the
contrast drawn by Paul between the flesh and the
spirit. As all students of Paulinism know, one of the
most difficult problems connected with its interpretation is to fix the meaning attached by Paul to the
term " the flesh." After devoting much attention to
this subject, I find myself unable to believe that
Paul meant to identify the flesh with the body, and
on the following grounds. Paul includes among works
of the flesh sins that are not physical in their char-

acter, especially sins of temper. Secondly, he uses
language with reference to the body which he could
not use with reference to the flesh. For him the flesh
is so irretrievably evil that there is nothing for it but
to be crucified and completely abolished; but the
body, which has been the servant of sin, may equally
become the servant of righteousness. It is the temple
of the Holy Ghost, and in its glorification redemption
finds its completion. Again, it was a commonplace
with him that even while a man was in the body he
might have ceased to be in the flesh. Lastly, if the
body is the evil power in man and the source of sin,
the natural inference would be that it should be
crushed into submission by the strictest austerity.
But Paul did not look for salvation from sin along the
lines of asceticism and starvation of physical impulses,
but expected it to come through faith in Christ. And
I have long felt that a strict logic would not have
stopped short with asceticism. Physical death would
have been heralded as the way of salvation, and there
would have been no reason why the extreme step of
suicide should have been regarded as reprehensible.
Accordingly I do not find it possible to agree with
those who claim the apostle as teaching that the seat
of sin is to be found in the body.

If, then, the seat of sin is not to be sought in the
body, where are we to place it? We must strike inward and find it at the very core of our being. Sin
has its roots in self-love. Self-love is a perfectly

natural and, indeed, commendable quality. The will to live, the instinct for self-preservation, the desire for self-gratification are implanted in us by Nature, which thus secures the preservation of the species as well as of the individual. It is therefore not wrong in itself. But it may readily become wrong if it collides with a higher law. Now in its essence sin arises from the collision of self-love with the will of God. We choose that which tends to gratify self even when it involves rebellion against our heavenly Father. It is self-assertion against God, of the creature against the Creator, of the child against the parent. The will of man clashes with the will of God.

The question arises, then, Why is it that in God's creatures there should be this disharmony with the Creator's will? And this problem is best discussed in connexion with the whole subject of the origin of sin. It has been usual to suppose that man's present condition testifies to the entrance of something abnormal into the life of the race. It is thought to exhibit the marks of disorder and ruin. Some sinister influence has poisoned the spring at its source, and his history has been set on lines other than those originally intended. Man was made upright at the first, but his nature has been warped, and the whole development has proceeded along false lines. Such is the ecclesiastical doctrine of the Fall, which has seemed to many theologians, in spite of its great difficulties, to be demanded by the explicit teaching of Scripture. The

Biblical evidence on which it is believed to rest is the story of Adam and Eve in Paradise, and the references to Adam in Romans and 1 Corinthians. It is, however, thought to be corroborated by another consideration, namely, that the universality of sin requires some such event to explain it. The assumption on which this conviction rests is that God cannot have created man as we find him—the tares in the cornfield cannot be of His sowing.

With reference to the story in Genesis, I would remark that theologians have now generally surrendered much that used to be drawn from it. In the first place, the extravagant language concerning the condition of Adam is now, by common consent, abandoned. The best known, perhaps, of these exaggerations is South's saying : "An Aristotle was but the rubbish of an Adam, and Athens but the rudiments of Paradise." No claims for marvellous intellectual endowment are now made for our first parents. Further, many theologians would now candidly admit a very large parabolic element in the story. That a few thousand years ago the human race came into existence as described in the second chapter of Genesis, and passed through the experience related in the third, is more than they are prepared to admit with their knowledge of science and of history. It is clear, then, that the foundations on which the current doctrine of man's original condition and his fall from it repose are, so far as the narratives in Genesis are concerned, in a very insecure condition. I would also point out that if we isolate this narrative and seek to interpret it without reading in ideas either of later Jewish theology or of the apostle Paul, we shall not find much support for the doctrine in question. There is nothing said of man's original righteousness, nor is there any hint that a new element emerged in the ethical constitution of man, nor yet that this element was transmitted to Adam's descendants.

The question, however, must be faced whether this doctrine is not involved in the teaching of Paul. On this I believe that there is widespread misapprehension. The question is very important, because at this point many believe that the definite breakdown of the Pauline Theology occurs. It is not unusual to hear that Paul's doctrine of salvation depends on his doctrine of sin, that his doctrine of sin depends on the assumption that the third chapter of Genesis is literal history, and that the bottom has been knocked out of this assumption by our modern knowledge, and that consequently the Pauline Theology collapses. I believe this chain of statements to be incorrect, and to rest upon serious misunderstanding as to the apostle's meaning. At present, however, I am concerned with his interpretation of the story in Genesis.

I freely grant at the outset that Paul treated the third chapter in Genesis as literal history. It would be unreasonable to expect anything else. The difficulties that we feel about it were not present to his mind, and he naturally shared the standpoint of his own countrymen with reference to it. But this, so far from diminishing the value of his discussion, to my mind only enhances it. For it is a sign of his remarkable insight into spiritual realities that he constructed his doctrine in such a way that it is intrinsically unaffected if we discard the historical character of the third chapter of Genesis. What interested him was not historical details, but spiritual principles, and these come clearly to light in the discussion which he gives to them.

In Romans v. 12–21 we have his most explicit treatment of the subject. It is true that he deals with the subject somewhat incidentally, his chief purpose being to set forth the greatness of the redemption achieved by Christ, and this he does by a parallel between Christ and Adam, which develops into a contrast. It would, however, be a mistake, in my judgment, to imagine that the incidental character of the exposition warranted us in inferring that his doctrine of Adam constituted an unimportant element in his teaching. I believe, on the contrary, that it was fundamental in his theology. The passage is singularly involved and difficult, and this makes it hard to be sure of its precise interpretation. We gain assistance in our attempt to understand it from our general reconstruction of Paul's theology, but especially from the parallel that he draws between Christ and Adam. Details which are obscure in one case sometimes grow much clearer through comparison with the other side of the parallel. It would involve minute exegetical discussion, such as would be quite unsuitable for a volume of this kind, to vindicate the conclusions to which a study of this passage has brought me. As, however, I do not wish to state results without some indication of processes, I shall try to suggest some reasons for the conclusions presented.

We are struck at the outset by the fact that Paul appears to trace the physical death of mankind both to the sin of Adam and to the sin of all. He says that through one man sin entered into the world, then, through the agency of sin, death followed, then death passed on to all men because all sinned. At first sight it seems that Paul does nothing more in this passage than assert that sin and death gained their foothold in the world through the act of Adam, and that the death of each individual was due, not to the sin of Adam, but to his own personal sin. I do not believe, however, that this is what Paul meant. It does not correspond to notorious facts, since it does not cover the case of infants who die before they attain a condition of moral responsibility. The tense of the Greek verb employed also suggests that Paul did not contemplate a series of acts lasting throughout the whole history of humanity and repeated in the case of each individual, but a single act taking place at a definite time. Moreover, the parallelism between Christ and Adam bids us seek a cause for universal death analogous to the cause of death's reversal. Now, it was not Paul's doctrine that the resurrection, which is the reversal of physical death, came to men in virtue of their own righteousness; it was achieved for them through the act of Christ. Accordingly we expect that the death of all will be ascribed by him, not to the personal sin of the individual, but to the sin of Adam.

And this conclusion is confirmed by Paul's language elsewhere. Thus he says, " As in Adam all die, so in Christ shall all be made alive." Here a direct relation is traced between Adam and the fact of universal death, which makes it probable that we must interpret in the light of this thought the passage we are discussing. Again, if we look at the way in which Paul proceeds we shall see that this interpretation is favoured by the immediate context, for Paul goes on to explain that while the generations from Adam until Moses had not been under the Law, and therefore could not be counted guilty of transgression, they nevertheless died. The obvious inference is that since death is due to sin, and no sin was imputed to them personally, their death was due to the sin of Adam. And when we look away from the immediate context to consider the passage as a whole, we must be struck by the fact that the emphasis lies entirely on the acts of Adam and Christ. So Paul speaks of the trespass of the one and the grace of the one man Jesus Christ, of condemnation resulting to all men through one trespass, and justification through one act of righteousness, of one man's disobedience through which many were constituted sinners, and the obedience of one through which many shall be made righteous.

The whole drift of the passage, then, as well as Paul's allusions elsewhere, convince me that he traces the death of all men to the act of Adam. What, then, are we to make of his assertion that death passed unto all men because all sinned ? If in the same breath he can trace universal death both to the sin of Adam and to the sin of all, the solution of this apparent contradiction is to be sought in the identification of the two. The sin of Adam is the sin of all. Thus we come by these purely exegetical considerations to the old theological formula that all sin in Adam.

The question, however, which immediately confronts us is this : In what sense are we to assert that the sin of Adam is the sin of all ? Frequently theologians have argued that all men were actually present in a sense in Adam, and therefore participated in his act to a certain extent, on the same principle on which Levi is said, in the Epistle to the Hebrews, to have done homage to Melchizedek in Abraham. But obviously a statement of that kind can carry no conviction to us. We cannot allow that unborn generations could participate in and be responsible for the act of their common ancestor. There would, indeed, be much more sense in saying that Adam was responsible for the sin of all his descendants than for saying that all his descendants participated in his sinful and guilty act.

I believe that we must seek for the explanation along quite other lines. We may illustrate Adam's relation to the race from the position held by the leader of a party who adopts a certain policy which meets with failure. The leader acts not in his private, but in a public capacity, and his party is committed by his acts. He stands as the representative of the principles by which the party is animated, and when he falls from power his party falls with him. This may serve as a rough illustration of the connexion between Adam and the race. We understand why all sin in Adam, if Adam acts as the representative of all. Now, this is meaningless except on the supposition that he acts as a true representative of humanity. Here, then, I am forced to diverge from the usual statement of the doctrine, for this rather implies that there was a marked difference between Adam's condition before his act of transgression and his condition after his act, a condition in which all his posterity have shared. My own belief is that Paul regarded the act of Adam as making no difference whatever to the ethical constitution of man. In other words, I interpret his doctrine that all sinned in Adam to mean that the act of Adam was rightly regarded as equivalent to the act of all, because it expressed a character common to himself and the race.

Such, I believe, to be the interpretation to which Paul's language, so far as we have at present stated it, would most naturally lead us. And when we consider what he says elsewhere it becomes very difficult to avoid this conclusion. For any one who will carefully consider what Paul has to say about Adam will be struck by the great difference between his utterances and the extravagant descriptions to which I have already referred. Here we have no picture of spacious intellect or assertion of moral grandeur. On the contrary, Paul carefully picks his terms in order to emphasise the low level of his metaphysical and ethical character. Adam became a living soul, whereas the second Adam became a life-giving spirit; the former was the natural, the latter the spiritual man; the first Adam sprang from the earth and was made of dust, the second Adam came from heaven. And not only has Paul this low view of Adam, but he places Adam and his posterity on the same footing. He says that "we have borne the image of the earthy," and "as is the earthy, so are they also that are earthy."

If, then, we assert that Adam is the representative of the race, not in virtue of his distinction from it, but of his community of nature with it, we must put to ourselves the question, In what does this ethical identity consist? I have never been able to reach any other conclusion than this, that Paul considered the flesh of Adam to be ethically constituted as our own. I have already discussed and set aside the view that when Paul spoke of the flesh he meant the body. What he did mean by it is a very difficult question. We may say, however, that in its specific sense it is substantially identical with what we call the carnal nature. It stands for all those qualities within us which are in antagonism to God and to righteousness. Now in ordinary experience the flesh is universally sinful, hence Paul speaks of it as " flesh of sin." When the Law comes to a man the sin that is latent within him springs up into life and becomes the dominating power within him. Of these three elements—the flesh, the law, and sin—the two latter were present in Adam. He, too, was under the commandment, and in his case also sin sprang into life. It is not an unnatural inference that in his case also the sinful flesh was present, and that thus his experience coincided with the experience repeated in the individual.

What, then, does the act of Adam become as thus interpreted ? It becomes a representative act ; it is not the caprice of an individual choice, that might conceivably have been different, with which we have in this case to do. It would obviously be difficult to defend the treatment of such an act as involving all mankind in sin. It is rather an act in which the whole moral character of the race stands revealed. Just because Adam is a sample of humanity his act is critical. It reveals man's sinful nature, and shows that under the stimulus of law transgression inevitably follows. The sin of all in Adam thus receives a worthy meaning quite different from the paltry ideas that have been popularly associated with it. If, then, I am right in thus interpreting Paul, man came into being with a sinful nature which woke to rebellion at the touch of the law. Till the law came he was innocent, but once there dawned upon him the consciousness of the moral order the life of innocence was broken up, the sinful nature found expression in the act of trespass, and innocence gave place to guilt. And as God looked upon it He saw the whole character of humanity clearly displayed, pronounced all men sinners, and imposed the penalty of physical death.

It will now be clear, I hope, that the whole of this great construction, while it is formally associated with the story of Adam, is really independent of it. For Paul's interest is not historical, but ethical and psychological. At whatever point we place the origin of the human race, or whatever name we might give to the first man, the central truth which Paul affirms remains. We cannot now, perhaps, draw sharp lines of demarcation and say, Here the non-moral passes into the moral, here the sinfulness latent in the nature finds expression, and innocence passes over into guilt. To the eye of God things are not blurred and indistinct as they are with ourselves.

So far, then, I have sought to interpret the Pauline doctrine of sin and show that it has been commonly misunderstood. The apostle gives no countenance to the view that the first act of transgression effected a fundamental change in man's ethical constitution. The sinful act was the outcome and expression of a sinful nature. It was a critical act in more senses than one, but not critical in the sense that it introduced a new element into human nature.

Not only, however, is the doctrine as commonly presented out of harmony with Paul's real meaning, but it is exposed to other serious objections. In the first place, we have the difficulty of accounting for a first sin occurring at all in the case of a sinless being. We cannot see, on the one hand, how such a being would of his own accord fall into sin. Why should he do something so abnormal, so contrary to the whole law of his nature? But, on the other hand, we are in no better position if we assume that the temptation came from without. This in a way increases rather than mitigates the difficulty, for now we have two problems to solve rather than one. If we take back the origin of human sin to the solicitations of a supernatural power, we have, first of all, to account for the evil qualities of the tempter, who is also a creature of God. We do not get rid of our perplexity by pushing it a stage further back. And in addition to this we have still the problem how an external solicitation can have met with a response in a sinless being. If sin came from without, there must have been some element in man to which it appealed.

In the next place we have the difficulty of imagining

that an act, however critical, should have such stupendous consequences. It might, no doubt, be urged that this is by no means unexampled. A few inches may make all the difference in the determination of a river's course. It may be just this side or just the other side of the watershed, and these few inches determine whether it is one country or another that is to be served by its waters. But this problem is much more complex, for it is not the history of an individual, but the history of humanity with which we are dealing. Let us suppose that the first man made a false start. We can understand how that might affect his whole future ; it might give a sinful bias to the whole of his life. But we have to account for a law affecting the whole of humanity, and we must seek for an explanation of the universal sinfulness of mankind.

We might be carried part of the way by a reference to the power of example without affirming any change in the moral constitution of man. The first man becoming himself a sinner might corrupt others by his evil example, and so all might grow up to imitate the evil actions of those about them. We have, of course, to recognise that there is no such thing in life, as we know it, as an individual isolated from a social environment, and this evil effect of environment no doubt accounts for much of the actual sin of the world. But a very slight reflection will show us that such a view would be too superficial. In the first place, it would by no means follow that evil example would inevitably be imitated. In the case we are supposing the ethical quality of each individual remains unaffected by the act of the first man, and, since that ethical character was in his case originally sinless, we must, on the hypothesis we are now considering, affirm a similar natural sinlessness for his successors. But on such a theory it is obvious that we have no right to anticipate that the evil example would be followed in every instance. One might rather anticipate quite the opposite. Hence it is clear that a reference to the power of example does not carry us far enough. For we can with certainty predict of each individual that as he comes to years of moral discernment the virus of sin will inevitably reveal itself in him. It is accordingly useless to appeal to a factor which is so inadequate to explain the phenomena. We are dealing here with a universal law, and we can argue infallibly from the invariable emergence of sin in human life to the universal sinfulness of human nature. This hypothesis accordingly must be set aside as insufficient.

The common doctrine of original sin also decisively recognises the unsatisfactoriness of this explanation. It emphasises very strongly that sin is a law of man's being, that it is woven into the texture of his nature, that as soon as the stage of responsibility is reached in each individual it is invariably manifested in sinful acts. But it accounts for this universal sinfulness of mankind not as an original quality of human nature, but as one introduced into it through the act of a single individual. He did not merely set a bad example, but he fundamentally changed, and changed for the worse, the character of the race. That a single act should have such far-reaching consequences is, I have already said, hard to believe, but the credibility of it is still more diminished when we try to think out the process. Ordinarily, I suppose, it would be explained in this way. The first act of transgression vitiated the moral nature of the first man. He handed on to his descendants a character irretrievably damaged, so that none of them have the option which he had before his transgression ; all are inevitably doomed to sin in consequence of his act. Two difficulties emerge here. The first is as to the change thus effected in the character of the first man, the other touches the transmission to his descendants of the vitiated nature. To the first of these I have already alluded, but the difficulty attached to the second is far greater.

It is not uncommon to invoke heredity as the explanation, but heredity is itself an extremely difficult and obscure subject, as to which eminent scientists assure us that very widespread misconceptions exist. We notice, of course, that things tend to run in families, as we say, that there is hereditary transmission of qualities from parent to child. But there is a marked tendency among scientists to restrict the scope of this principle within much narrower limits than the layman assigns to it. We have here the

K

following points to observe. First, the question of original sin touches not simply the physical, but the spiritual side of man. Secondly, how far can the principle of heredity cover both of these factors? Thirdly, with what confidence may we believe that heredity is able to respond to the task that is here thrown upon it? I begin with the last of these.

Most of us are, perhaps, familiar with the fact that there is a great controversy in the ranks of experts as to the transmission by heredity of acquired characteristics. The individual may transmit to his descendants physical qualities that were born with him; but if he subsequently acquires a characteristic, it is believed by an influential school of biologists that he cannot hand this on to his descendants. This is, of course, a matter for the experts, and it would be absurd for any one who has no competence in such matters to express any opinion. But the bearing of the dispute on our problem is obvious. Even granting the large assumption that the first man's nature acquired these new characteristics, there is very grave doubt whether such acquired characteristics could be transmitted to his descendants by heredity. But granting, for the sake of argument, that they could, we are only at the beginning of our difficulties. For it is the physical qualities which are thus transmitted, whereas our question has even more to do with the ethical and spiritual change. No doubt the physical counts for a good deal. The man who said that he found it easier to get the devil out of his heart than his grandfather out of his bones embodied in a crude epigram an element of truth. The physical nature often accounts for much in this respect, but, as I have already pointed out, it does not account for everything, nor, indeed, for the most vital things. The seat of sin is not in the body, but in the spirit, and it may be gravely questioned whether heredity helps us in the slightest here. I do not propose to enter into the thorny discussion of traducianism and creationism, but a word or two is inevitable at this point. Theologians have been split into hostile camps on the question of the origin to be assigned to the spiritual part of the individual. The traducianists conceived it to be propagated like the body, the creationists regarded each spirit as the direct and immediate creation of God. A third possible view which has been held by some eminent Christian theologians, notably by Origen and Julius Müller, is the theory of pre-existence. The complexity of the problem is, of course, increased by the extremely intimate relations between body and spirit. Nevertheless, I believe that the great majority of theologians at the present day would decidedly reject the view that the spirit is propagated along with the body. The coarse materialism of such a conception is quite alien from our more refined way of looking at things. It is therefore very hard to say how the act of the first ancestor could have affected at all directly the spiritual nature of his descendants.

If neither example nor heredity suffice as the explanation, to what are we driven? A possible view would be to regard the depravity of the race as due to the mere determination of God, who visited the original transgression with this consequence. This, however, while logically possible, is surely morally unthinkable. That God, who loathes and hates sin, should deliberately set Himself to pervert human character in the way described would be something wholly unworthy of Him.

Accordingly we seem to be driven back to the view of Paul that the initial transgression was the consequence and not the cause of human sinfulness. No doubt the reluctance to admit this has been largely due to the consequences which it is supposed to involve. It is often thought that with the disappearance of the usual doctrine of sin the doctrine of the Atonement also disappears. This, however, is incorrect. The need of redemption rests not upon the hypothetical first sin, but upon the universal dominion of sin in human life. The urgent question, it is well said, is not how sin came into the world, but how we can get it out, and this practical question remains, whatever conclusion we reach on the speculative problem.

Another difficulty is that it is hard to believe in the sinfulness of the first man, since it is supposed that God would create him sinless. But I would point out that the same problem arises in connexion with the individual. The innocent child comes to us fresh, we might say, from the hand of God, and yet we all know that no sooner has the age of moral consciousness been attained than with it there comes the experience of sin. The difficulty is really no greater in the case of one than in the case of the other. But no doubt what is in people's minds, further, is that here there is quite a new beginning, that there were not, as in the case of the child, antecedents which might explain its fall from innocence. It is here, however, that our modern way of looking at things makes a difference. We do not recognise the absolute new beginning now as our predecessors did. We make room for the evolutionary theory of the origin of mankind. This is not to say that Theology is pinned down to any particular form of that theory. All that I mean is that we must leave room for the view that a long animal past lies behind us. Now, this at once throws a new and welcome light on several sides of the problem.

In the first place it provides us with an explanation of the origin of sin which, while it may not account for everything, accounts, nevertheless, for much. We see man beginning his career with the instincts of ferocity and cruelty, greed and selfishness and cunning, stamped deeply into his organism, transmitted to him by innumerable animal ancestors. As these existed in the animal they were not sinful. We cannot, without an abuse of language, speak of the animal as moral or immoral; he is simply non-moral. But there comes a time when man appears. We perhaps could not put our finger on the fine line which separates one from the other, but Nature does move forward at times by leaps, and those of us who believe in the ever-present action of the living God will have no difficulty in believing that, however fine the line might appear to us, it was nevertheless critical; the Rubicon was irretrievably crossed—man starts on his upward career. But he starts heavily handicapped, the animal qualities remain in all their strength, and all that can be at present pitted against them is the faint consciousness of moral distinction which has just struggled to its birth. Yet in that feeble sense of right and wrong lay much of the hope of man's stupendous moral progress. We cannot wonder that the weak moral consciousness made but little headway against the overwhelming mass of inherited impulse.

But not only does sin emerge with the consciousness of moral distinctions, but, as Paul has taught us, the recognition of a moral order brings not merely the consciousness of sin, but acts even as an incitement to its commission. For when the impulse which hitherto has acted without check feels the sense of a new restraint, the inevitable result is that a feeling of irritation springs up in man against this unwelcome intruder. The irksome restriction chafes him, and the Law becomes the strength of sin. Hence a new phenomenon appears. He not only does the same acts as his animal progenitors, but he does them with a new intensity, and not simply for the sake of gratifying his impulses, but for the sake of doing them, just because they are forbidden by his better self. In other words, we have a new element of rebellion appearing, the deliberate thwarting of the higher law by self-will.

Sin may thus be regarded as on one side an anachronism, to use a term which has been applied to it, as the survival from a lower stage into a higher. What was harmless and natural on the animal plane becomes mischievous and wrong on the human plane. We may even say that it is unnatural, for although the instincts are there and their gratification is, in one sense, natural, yet the true destiny of man is to live in harmony with the higher law of his being. A difference is made when the physical elements in the animal become the physical elements in man, and he violates his own nature when he subordinates the higher to the lower. But it is more than a mere anachronism. We cannot split man into two disconnected parts and treat either as independent of the other. We cannot adopt the maxim of some Gnostics: "The jewel is untarnished though the casket lie in the mire." For the relationship between spirit and body is not the relationship of jewel and casket. There is a mutual interpenetration of the two, and the self as we know it is not spirit which has a body, but a combination of the two. If a man gets drunk, it might be argued that he is seeking simply a physical gratification in which his spiritual part does not participate. But that is incorrect. The gratification which his body enjoys is *his* gratification; it is something in which the whole self participates.

It may, of course, be questioned whether this gives a sufficient account of sin. I have already pointed out that the seat of sin is not in the body, and that many sins are entirely independent of a physical organisation. It might accordingly be argued that, while the animal passions derived from our prehuman past explain our physical sins, there is much which they do not explain. This may be true, and I do not profess to give a complete account of what is probably an insoluble mystery. But if we set ourselves to think out what happens when self-gratification in the case of intellectual and moral beings comes in collision with a higher law, it is not difficult to see how several other forms of sin may arise. Moreover, we must not forget that non-physical sins as well as physical have their prototypes in the animal world.

Finally, this view is a real help to us when we come to consider the problem of evil as it affects God. On this I have spoken in an earlier chapter, but it is necessary to touch on the question here, in spite of the repetition it involves. The old dilemma that God is either not good or He is not all-powerful does not now come to us with the same force. It would be hard for us to understand how God should create a creature at the human stage so liable to evil that he fell before the first breath of temptation. But when we see that God has deliberately chosen to create man by the method of evolution, that He has worked by development rather than by sudden catastrophe, we understand how inevitable it was that, under these conditions, things should have taken the course they did. The theory of special creation may no doubt seem preferable to some ; my own view is that the other is the worthier way.

It may still be urged, however, that evil first emerged in the spiritual universe, where this explanation is out of place, and that we must, if we are to clear God's character, find another way. I would repeat, in reply to this, that even God cannot have a thing and not have it at the same time. There is no value in compulsory goodness ; it can be of value only where the will is free, and therefore God had the alternatives either to endow His creatures with freedom of choice or to create automata, or to abstain from creation altogether. To have accepted either of the latter alternatives would have been to confess defeat, to have excluded the possibility of freely rendered obedience, lest obedience should be freely withheld. Therefore He took the risk of failure, which was the price of the possibility of success. And since He is not fickle or capricious, when He deliberately adopted a certain course of conduct He had to go forward with it and accept the inevitable consequences of His choice.

It may be urged, however, Granted that God accepts this risk, yet if what you say is true, the method He adopted in the case of man involved not simply the risk, but the certainty of failure. And if so, can we really speak of sin when the dice are so loaded that the game must always be lost? The difficulty is a real one, and I cannot pretend to explain why sin is inevitable, and yet man is to blame for it. But I would point out that precisely the same difficulty is presented by our everyday experience. We all recognise that sin is inevitable for every individual, yet, at the same time, we regard this sin as blameworthy, and, with regard to the single action, we say in each case, This might have been avoided; I am to blame for doing it.

I am conscious that what I have said seems very inadequate, but no one has succeeded in reaching a satisfactory answer. We are here in a region of contradictories. Still, suggestions may remain which are helpful so far as they go, and I think that the view which I have put forward finds support in the profound and far-reaching words with which Paul closes his great discussion of national election: "God has shut up all unto disobedience that He might have mercy upon all."

CHAPTER VIII

DOES IT MATTER IF THE GOSPEL HISTORY IS UNTRUE ?

FOR the religious unrest of our age there are not a few who are inclined to believe that it is the ntimate connexion of Christianity with history that is really to blame. Here, we are told, is the Achilles' heel of the orthodox theologies. It is here that they lay themselves open to attack which is likely to prove fatal. For if we vitally connect the truths of religion with certain events that happened in time and space we at once raise the question, Did those events really happen or not ? And when we raise a question of this kind we have to settle it by critical methods, and thus we at once expose the truth of our religion to the perils of historical research ; and if we reach the result that the alleged events did not happen, then it will go hard with the claim of the religion to be true. How much better it would be, we are exhorted, if we dissolved the alliance between the Gospel and history, and threw our stress on those ideas which are independent of events in time and space. With one clean cut we should escape the embarrassments which the entanglement imposes upon us. It is tempting to purchase freedom from entangling complications, but we may buy our liberty at too dear a price.

There can, indeed, be no doubt that from some points of view the prospect thus held out to us is an alluring one. To soar away from the dreary earth into the rare atmosphere of beautiful ideas, to reach that peaceful region where we are no longer in the rough and tumble of historical controversy, to have gone where critics cease from troubling, that would be a delightful experience. How exhilarating to be borne upward and upward on the bold, unfettered wing of pure speculation till we have scaled the cloudy ramparts and found ourselves at home in the city of eternal truth!

Moreover, it must be confessed that the disadvantages of our alliance with history are no figment of the imagination. Once we have laid stress upon historical events as vital to our position, we cannot warn the critic off. Where history is, the critic has the right to come. If you say, these facts must be accepted as an integral part of the religion, then the historicity of the facts is a matter for investigation which we have no right to shirk. Once the question has been raised, it must be answered. And all who know anything of the processes of historical research are familiar with the difficulties and uncertainties that inevitably attend it. An event in past history must be attested to us by documentary evidence. This evidence must be examined by the methods of inquiry appropriate to the subject. The documents must be critically examined, the scholar must seek to discover their date, their authorship, their place of origin, and whether they incorporate older documents. If he comes to the conclusion that these older documents are present, he must seek, as far as possible, to disengage them and restore them to their original form. If he finds conflicting versions of the same event, he must attempt by a process of comparison to work back to the earlier stage of the tradition from which both originated. He must, however, not only investigate the documents in which the story has come down to him ; he must examine the intrinsic credibility of the story itself. He may find that on investigation it breaks down, or, on the other hand, it may successfully pass through all the tests to which he exposes it. Or, as is often the case, he may find that several details in the story break down, but that the story itself in its main outline remains unshaken. Such an inquiry has obvious risks. If it be free, and any other type of investigation is worthless, then it must have an open mind with reference to its possible results. The chance of unfavourable decision must inevitably be taken. Let us not delude ourselves with the idea that we can stop when we are half through. Thoroughness and fearlessness must be the badge of those who are servants of truth. Ought we, then, to listen to those seductive voices that tell us how much better we should be if we would give up troubling about the facts and place all our emphasis on the ideas?

I believe that it would be fatal to do so. We do not want the religion of cloudland, but the religion of concrete life, of human experience and emotion based solidly upon the earth. It is not a new thing by any means to cut religion loose from history and to dissipate the facts of the Gospel into fine abstract ideas. But we ought not to disguise from ourselves that a Christianity disentangled from the Gospel facts has ceased to be Christianity in any real sense of the term. There are other religions in which ideas play the supreme part. Their founders have been great teachers, such as Zoroaster or Gautama. The religions they proclaimed or the ethical systems they inculcated were quite independent of the teacher himself. He was just a prophet, and had the words that he spoke been uttered by others their validity would not have been in the least affected, nor does any alleged event in their life have any vital relation to the system they founded. It is different with Christianity. It stands or falls not by the truth of its ideas merely, but even more by the truth of its facts—not, it is true, by all the facts narrated in the Gospel history. Many of these are not vital to the existence of Christianity, even though they may be important in themselves, and a Christian may be very unwilling to let them go. But there are certain facts which are really vital, and cannot be surrendered without a surrender of the

Gospel itself. Prominent among these facts is the Incarnation of the Son of God in the Person of Jesus of Nazareth, and as a corollary from that the tremendous significance of His work in the world culminating in His death and resurrection. In other words Christianity sinks or swims with the assertion that at a certain period of time a human personality appeared on the stage of history and was the incarnate Son of God. If that is gone, there is much that is left which is valuable, it is true. There is left the teaching of Jesus, especially on the Fatherhood of God, and all which flows out of that. Whether He or another spoke the great moral and religious utterances which are to be found in our Gospels, the sayings themselves abide. It would therefore be incorrect to say that if the view of the Church about Jesus is untrue, then the New Testament contains nothing worth having. But, all the same, it would cease to be Christianity as the term has come to be understood. True, we should have the exhibition of a very elevated character in the New Testament portrait of Jesus. We should have a series of religious aphorisms and a set of religious parables unrivalled in the literature of the world. But we should not have the manifestation of God in human life, the supreme exhibition of His grace and forgiving love, the redemptive energy, the power for the conquest of sin and creation of a holy life, which, if Christianity is true, are present within it. We must take the risk of an inseparable alliance with history if we do not want the religion to lose the qualities that make Christianity supremely precious.

And it would be a short-sighted policy for another reason. We may soar from the earth to cloudland congratulating ourselves that history has no wings to follow us. But not only do we leave behind us at history's mercy our most valuable possessions that our upward flight may not be impeded, but even in cloudland we are not safe. For if history cannot follow us, philosophy can and will. If we say it is no matter whether the alleged events happened or not, we are no longer hit by a demonstration that they never happened at all, but we have still to run the gauntlet of the criticism that the ideas the religion embodies are untrue. You stake your existence on ideas rather than on facts, but you are only out of the frying-pan into the fire. For when Philosophy comes to investigate your ideas, she is rather more likely than not to pronounce them untrue. Do what you will, it will probably remain true till the end of time that the Cross is to the Greeks foolishness. We shall be like the man of whom Amos tells us, who from the blistering heat outside " went into the house and leaned his hand on the wall, and a serpent bit him." For, after all, the fact that our ideas are very beautiful and comforting does not prove them to be true, and the result of jettisoning the facts as if they were unnecessary has vitally imperilled the ideas. For one of the great arguments for the truth of the ideas is just this, that they are guaranteed by the historical facts, and if we let the facts go the case of the ideas is likely to become parlous indeed. What it would be difficult for us to accept as true for its own sake we may confidently receive on the strength of the credentials with which it comes. For example, a belief in the love of God, in spite of its attractiveness, is one that it is very difficult to accept in face of the pain and misery we see everywhere about us. But the Christian appeals to history to vindicate him in his assurance of God's love. It is because he believes not simply in the teaching of Jesus, but in the fact of Jesus as attesting the teaching, that his trust in God's love is unshaken. Many would be forced into pessimism were it not for their belief in Jesus.

I do not believe, therefore, that this is one of the points on which we can compromise. As I have already said, I freely grant that there are elements in the Gospel story which Christianity has no vital interest in asserting. It may have an interest in asserting them, but it is not vital. In other words, if they turn out to be untrue, the truth of Christianity itself will remain unaffected. But there are some things which lie at the very centre of the Christian position; cut those out, and Christianity has been eviscerated; its beating heart that drove the tides of life through every member of Christ's body has been taken away; and that which constituted the very life of the Church and all its redemptive energy

L

ceases to carry forward its mighty and beneficent work.

But it is by no means uncommon to find ardent Christians who, while they would not dream of denying the Gospel history, nevertheless depreciate the importance of the historical Jesus. They throw such stress upon the living Christ, with whom they have immediate fellowship, that they grow indifferent and cold to the life recorded for us in the Gospels. The danger of this attitude is that those who yield to it fashion a Christ after their own fancy, and by so doing impoverish their own religious life. After all, to be quite honest with ourselves, the best way to know what the living Christ is will always, during our earthly life, be for us to know what the historical Jesus was. The story of the kite that snapped its string in the endeavour to break away from its control and soar upward with unimpeded flight, and pitched headlong to the earth, contains a warning for us. If we chafe against history as the cord which ties our soaring spirits to the earth, we are likely to find that if we snap our cord we also may plunge downwards from the heights it enables us to attain. Let us hold fast, then, to the living Christ, but with equal firmness to the Jesus of history. When eminent religious teachers stake the truth of Christianity on the testimony of the religious consciousness, and say that this in itself is enough, though criticism do its worst against the New Testament, one may well stand aghast at the recklessness of such a position. The Christian consciousness is a very complex thing ; it is rooted in certain historical facts guaranteed to us by the New Testament history, and conditioned throughout very largely by New Testament teaching. Cut the New Testament away, and sooner or later the Christian consciousness will vanish with it.

CHAPTER IX

CAN WE TRUST THE GOSPEL PORTRAIT
OF JESUS?

IN the preceding chapter I have argued that Christianity differs from other great religions in the position which it accords to its Founder. Had Jesus of Nazareth been simply a great teacher, the truth of His religion would not have been very intimately connected with the views that were entertained about Him by His followers. For then what was all-important would have been the message, and the truth and value of the religion would have been bound up with it alone. It would be a matter of comparative indifference whether the alleged author of the teaching had ever lived or not, or, if he had lived, whether he had uttered the words attributed to him. The teaching would be judged on its own merits. But that has never been the position adopted by Christians with reference to the Founder of their religion. He is an integral part of the religion. Eliminate Him, and, while much that is precious is left, that which is most precious has vanished away. For His greatest contribution to religion was not His doctrine of the Fatherhood of God, His estimate of the worth of the individual, His teaching about the Kingdom of God, or anything that He said at all. His supreme contribution to religion was Himself, His own personality, what He was and what He did. We belittle Him when we think of Him as merely the Teacher or as the Founder of the religion. He is not so much its Founder as its Foundation. And if our views of Him were to be radically changed, we should no longer be Christians in the fullest sense of the term.

But in our own day the helpless perplexity in which many are involved leaves little untouched. As it affects our present discussion, it takes the form of the question, Did such a person as Jesus of Nazareth ever exist, and, if so, have we any certain information about Him? Is the character correctly delineated, or is it idealised by followers who saw Him through a glorious haze of reverence and love? I begin, then, with the evidence for the existence of Jesus. In the first place, it is worth while pointing out that all expert New Testament scholars are agreed upon this point. This applies to those whose treatment of the history of Primitive Christianity is of the most radical and negative kind. Even those who have denied the authenticity of every single book in the New Testament have, as a rule, refused to take the further step of denying the historical existence of Jesus. The Dutch scholar Loman, it is true, did so at one time, but he subsequently withdrew his denial. Van Manen, who also denied the authenticity of the Pauline

Epistles, accepted as an historical fact the existence, not of Paul only, but of Jesus. It must be observed that many of these scholars had no prepossessions in favour of tradition. On the contrary, they broke with it in the most decisive way, yet they were convinced that it was not possible to eliminate the Person of Jesus from history.

I have said that history comes to us through documentary channels, and that criticism must begin by testing the authenticity of the documents. It would, of course, be impossible to give any full account of New Testament criticism at this point ; I must content myself with the following observations. I have mentioned that there are some scholars who have gone so far as to assert that Paul wrote none of the letters which have come to us under his name. These scholars, however, are extremely few, and not one of them can be said to belong to the first rank. The great names of advanced criticism, such as F. C. Baur, Strauss, Keim, Holsten, Holtzmann, Pfleiderer, Lipsius, Weizsäcker, Harnack, Schmiedel, and Wellhausen, have had no doubt whatever as to the authenticity of several of these Epistles. If any man can read the Epistles to the Corinthians and Galatians without feeling that they throb with the personality of the author and deal with actual historical situations full of actual human interest, he must be gravely deficient in a true feeling for history. Criticism has, in fact, steadily moved back towards tradition, so that, while

Baur accepted only four Epistles of Paul, the advanced critics of to-day usually recognise seven, several accept nine, and some go so far as to admit ten of these Epistles to be authentic. Let us see what this means. If we left only Baur's four Epistles standing amid the wreck—Romans, Corinthians, and Galatians —we should have indubitable evidence concerning Jesus from one who was His contemporary and knew His brother and His most eminent apostles, who was at first a fanatical opponent of the new movement, and later became its most powerful advocate. His letters attest the existence of Jesus and several facts in His career which are frequently alluded to in a quite incidental way, presupposing that the readers were already familiar with some of the details in the story of His life, death, and resurrection. The recognition of even one of these Epistles settles this question completely. But we are not left simply to these.

The criticism which has been busy with the Pauline Epistles has concerned itself also with the gospels. Here, again, the return to tradition, while not so marked as in the case of the Pauline Epistles, has still been significant. It is true that the tendency of advanced criticism is strongly to deny the Johannine authorship of the Fourth Gospel, and to set it aside as of little value for its information on the facts of Christ's life. But even here the tendency has been to push the date of the Gospel back to the early years of the second century—roughly speaking, half a century earlier than the date to which Baur assigned it. And the main part of the Synoptic Gospels must be considerably earlier, since their tradition is constantly presupposed in the Fourth Gospel. What is known as the Two-Document Theory is now very widely, though not universally, accepted. This theory is that two documents lie at the base of our Synoptists. One of them was either our Gospel of Mark or a document very much like it. This was employed by the authors of the first and third Gospels. That Mark was the earliest of the Gospels, and was employed by the authors of the other two, is the one fixed point which has been secured through the long investigations into the Synoptic Problem. The question as to the other sources is not answered with unanimity, but by far the most generally accepted view is that Matthew and Luke employed, in addition to Mark, another document which contained a large number of discourses of Jesus. Whether it consisted predominantly of discourses, or whether it contained a considerable proportion of narrative, and whether it was used by Mark in the composition of his Gospel, are points as to which the defenders of the Two-Document Theory are not agreed. In any case, we have to allow for a fairly complicated literary process which must have taken some time, and although it is not possible to reconstruct with certainty our lost second source, yet by a comparison of Matthew and Luke we can get back to a stage earlier than that represented by either of these Gospels. Much of this tradition must, on grounds of purely literary and historical criticism, have taken shape while hundreds who had known Jesus personally were still alive.

When we pass, however, from the question of documents to the narratives which they contain, we are led to take a favourable view of much that they tell us. In the first place, we may note the harmony of the character which they depict. We have a combination of numerous elements. In addition to the two main documents we are obliged to postulate other sources to account for the matter that is peculiar to Matthew or to Luke. Yet we are not conscious of any sense of incongruity as we move from section to section of the Gospel story. We cannot account for the Evangelists' figure of Jesus as the creation of unconscious art or the product of the mythicising faculty of the human mind. For without the concrete personality round which the myth could grow, we should have expected quite divergent representations to grow up in different circles. That several sources unite to give one portrait proves that they are reproducing the same original, and not leaving a fancy uncontrolled by reality to work its own will.

It may be said, however, that we have not to do with unconscious myth, but with deliberate invention. That, however, is not possible for several reasons. The best judges of character, those who have the widest familiarity with the creations of human genius, unite in confessing the peerless excellence of Jesus as presented to us in the Synoptic Gospels. Are we to suppose that some one sat down to invent a figure of this kind? We may well imagine what would have been the result. In the first place, such an artificial character would have been stiff and wooden, it would not and could not have moved with the exquisite grace and naturalness of the central figure in the Synoptists. In the next place, we have no reason to suppose that there was a transcendent genius among the early Christians who was capable of a literary and psychological feat of this kind. Once more, it is obvious that the very attempt to depict a perfect character from imagination would have defeated itself. For we are all creatures of our own time and nationality, incapable of breaking loose from the ideals which have become a very part of us. Now, it would have been inevitable in such an attempt that those features should have been most strongly emphasised which were most congenial to its author's ideas of perfection. But ideals change as we move from age to age, from country to country, from race to race, and an invented figure would have been stamped deeply with the limitations of his creator's age and nationality, with his personal predilections and prejudices. But how different it is with the Jesus of the Gospels. Perhaps the most striking characteristic of the figure is its universality —its timelessness. He appeals to all ages and is welcomed in all climes; everywhere it is felt that in Him humanity received its supreme expression, and that He embodies the perfection of the moral and spiritual ideal.

Once more, the figure cannot have been invented, since there are elements in the story which there was a great temptation to suppress. The early Christians venerated Jesus as Divine, and their temptation was to suppress such elements as might seem to a narrow and timid faith to be incompatible with the claims they made for Him. But there are several elements in the Gospel history which never could have been fabricated just because they created such difficulties for Christians. Such sayings as, "Why callest thou me good? None is good save one, that is God," or, "My God, my God, why hast Thou forsaken me?" or the assertion that He did not know the day of His Second Advent, it would never have occurred to any Christian to invent. They would never have emphasised His human frailty, nor would they have represented Him as owing His baptism to John the Baptist. The Evangelists had no temptation to invent the story that His own family thought Him mad. And why should they have created gratuitous difficulties by their stories of gradual cure, or by fabricating as a charge levelled against Him that He wrought His miracles by the help of Beelzebub? We may be thankful, indeed, that these and other elements have been preserved, not simply for their intrinsic importance, but as guaranteeing to us the reality of the personality.

And just as little as imperfect man could have created a perfect figure, so little could he have invented His teaching. It is quite easy to trace points of contact between that teaching and the systems of other masters. But what is significant is not the details, but the system as a whole, and no parallel to this can be found anywhere. That teaching is not an artificial combination of elements scraped together from this quarter or from that, it is the expression of the greatest religious genius the world has known.

Lastly, I wish to call attention to an argument which I stated in my lecture, " Did Jesus Rise Again ? " This was to the effect that no Jew could have concocted the story that the alleged Founder of his sect had been crucified. I believe myself that he would not have invented the story that He had been killed, but since some scholars believe that the Jews had developed the doctrine of a suffering Messiah by the first century I do not press this point, though I do not share their opinion. Those who are under the influence of Dr. Frazer's theories as developed in *The Golden Bough* may be inclined to think that heathen influence helped to create the story of the death of Jesus, and some hasty and injudicious readers have come to the conclusion that Dr. Frazer's argument justifies them in throwing aside a belief in the historical existence of Jesus altogether. Dr. Frazer is nowhere, I believe, so unconvincing as where he discusses the Passion story. But in case any who have drawn this illegitimate inference may read this chapter, I put on record a statement made in his latest volume, *Adonis, Attis, Osiris:* " The historical reality both of Buddha and of Christ has sometimes been doubted or denied. It would be just as reasonable to question the historical existence of Alexander the Great and Charlemagne on account of the legends which have gathered round them. The great religious movements which have stirred humanity to its depths and altered the beliefs of nations, spring ultimately from the conscious and deliberate efforts of extraordinary minds, not from the blind unconscious co-operation of the multitude. The attempt to explain history without the influence of great men may flatter the vanity of the vulgar, but it will find no favour with the philosophic historian."

But while it is conceivable that a Jew may have devised the story that the alleged Founder had been put to death, he could not have asserted that he was crucified, for crucifixion was a death which involved its victim in the curse of the Law. It is incredible that any adherent of the new sect should have created this strange story of a crucified, and therefore accursed, Messiah, and thus placed a gratuitous and almost insuperable obstacle in the path of Jews whom he invited to accept His religion. And how much assent could He have expected to receive from Gentiles, to whom the Cross was a death of infamy, the characteristic punishment of slaves ? We know what the

Messianic belief of Judaism was, and from it there can never have come the belief in a crucified Messiah. Only one explanation can be given for this abnormal development, namely, that death by crucifixion had overtaken One whom His followers regarded as Messiah, and whom, in spite of it, they persisted in regarding as Messiah. Just as surely as Adams and Le Verrier could infer the existence of Neptune before it was discovered, from the aberrations of Uranus, so surely from this strange deflexion of Jewish Messianism we can infer the crucifixion of Jesus of Nazareth.

CHAPTER X

THE MIRACLES OF JESUS

IN the preceding chapter I have sought to show that, our enemies themselves being judges, we have abundant reason to believe in the historical existence of Jesus of Nazareth. But we have gained much more than this conclusion. We have seen that there is good ground to believe that we have a series of documents written by the most eminent of the early Christian leaders, who had been a bitter enemy and persecutor of the movement before he became its strenuous adherent. These Epistles of Paul of Tarsus not simply abundantly prove the existence of Jesus of Nazareth, but they give us some highly important information about Him. For reasons that I do not now stay to discuss, they concentrate attention upon the Passion history, but they have numerous incidental al usions which throw light on the career, the character, and the teaching of the Founder. In these respects, however, we are far better informed in the narratives that compose our Synoptic Gospels, narratives which are early in date and contain many things which there was no temptation to invent. Hence we secure not s mply the bare historicity of a Messianic

Leader and the belief that His career culminated on the Cross, but we have a large amount of information which the vast majority of critics who are bound by no adherence to tradition would admit to be genuine historical reminiscence.

These documents, however, are viewed with reserve by a large number of modern scholars, because they contain narratives of miraculous events. The modern mind has largely ceased to believe in miracles, and it is not unnatural that the scepticism entertained with reference to miracles in general should be extended to the Gospel history. Accordingly we are confronted at this point with the problem presented by these narratives. At an earlier period it was usual to base the defence of Christianity very largely upon the miracles. Now, many feel them to be a hindrance to belief rather than a help. Perhaps we ought not to be so timid in our apologetic. It is true that we do not suspend the truth of Christianity by this single argument; but miracles have still their place in the evidence. Their relation to Christianity is twofold. One miracle, at least, is an integral part of Christianity; while it is at the same time an important element in the proof. But if miracles are used to prove Christianity, it may also be said that the character of Christianity makes its miracles more credible. Nor is this an argument in a circle. If it were said: We believe in the miracles because they are a part of Christianity, and proceeded: We believe in Christianity because it is demonstrated by the miracles, such an argument would be circular, and therefore worthless. But really the case is quite different. Both positions rest upon independent proof—Christianity on other proof than miracles, and miracles on the testimony to their actual occurrence. But the independent demonstration is confirmed in each case by the other. If Christianity is true, the Christian miracles become more credible, for they harmonise so perfectly with the religion, and find in it a worthy justification ; and if the miracles are true, we have a valuable endorsement of the claim of Christianity to be a supernatural revelation. It will be convenient, however, to speak of the evidence for the miracles at this point ; for unquestionably, if their historical character can be established, they constitute a strong presumption in favour of the truth of Christianity.

The first consideration to which I would draw attention is that critics are now generally prepared to admit a larger element of fact in narratives which lie outside the range of common experience. This is particularly the case with the narratives of healing, which are now regarded as historical in the main, though the incidents are not treated as miraculous. This applies also to the cure of those who are spoken of as demoniacs in the Gospel narrative. Not, of course, that those who reject miracles would believe in demon-possession, but that they would treat the maladies which they regard as thus incorrectly diag-

M

nosed by the evangelist as real maladies specially susceptible to mind-cure. Our increasing recognition of what we commonly call the action of mind on matter has made it possible for them to believe in much which their predecessors would have scouted without hesitation. It is quite possible that ere long these concessions may be extended to other miracles. Yet it is questionable whether extension along these lines will ever cover the whole of the cases with which we have to deal. What attitude, then, are we to take up with reference to the miracles strictly so called ?

At the outset it is necessary to insist, because it is often ignored, that to justify belief in a miracle the evidence needs to be exceptionally strong. It is sometimes said that if we refuse to believe in miracles, we might just as well refuse to believe in any history. But the fact is that when we read narratives of miracles in secular historians we instinctively and without any hesitation do disbelieve them ; while, apart from grave reasons to the contrary, we accept the account they give us of ordinary events. And rightly, for we feel that we need something more than mere assertion to warrant our belief. The evidence is strong enough to bear the weight of events which do not diverge from the order of Nature, but under the strain of miracles it hopelessly breaks down. And we cannot object to the demand that the evidence for the Christian miracles should be very strong and satisfy very rigorous tests. Nor can there be any doubt that within the last fifty years the prejudice against any belief in miracles has become much more intense. The universal reign of Law and the uniformity of Nature have been emphasised by science, and caprice has been steadily driven from the field. Great objection is felt to any interference with the normal order, such as might induce an uneasy feeling that the course of Nature could not be relied on. At all hazards, it is felt, our trust in the consistency of Nature must not be put to confusion. The attempts to parry this objection have been various and of unequal merit. It has been pointed out that the law of uniformity is only an inference from observation of what has actually happened, and that logically we have no right to assume that what has uniformly happened in the past is the law for what is yet to happen. If this were a matter of mere logic, such a criticism would be valid. But we all have a fixed conviction, on which we habitually act, that the course of Nature will proceed to-morrow as it did yesterday, and that the reign of law will not be displaced by that of topsy-turvydom. We should think a man mad if he told us that the sun might rise in the west, or that streams would begin to run uphill, or that water would freeze if we raised its temperature to boiling point. We have an invincible confidence that we shall have no irrational surprises of this kind, but may fully trust that the same causes will continue to produce the same effects. Nor can we derive much help from the suggestion that in the original constitution of the universe provision was made for the sudden emergence of miracle. Babbage showed that a calculating machine could be invented which should proceed for a long series of calculations on a given principle, then suddenly work according to a different principle altogether, and again revert to its first method. Any one who had watched its action for a hundred thousand times would feel that he had irresistible evidence for believing that he had mastered the law of the machine, and that as long as it worked it would work in that way. But unknown to him a principle would have been embodied in the machine which, when it came into operation, would prove the alleged law to be a complete mistake. Now logically, of course, we might apply this principle to the universe. We have only observed its working over a comparatively brief period, and all the so-called laws of Nature are merely based upon our observation during that period. It is possible that the universe might have been made on principles similar to that of Babbage's machine. In that case a point might be reached at which new forces should come into operation, changing the conditions in what would seem to be a miraculous manner, yet in perfect harmony with the law of its being.

I do not think, however, that much help is to be gained along these lines. For one thing, the most ardent believer in miracles will not expect to see the customary order of Nature radically reversed. He believes in its rationality and order too much for that. Moreover, we do not regard the universe as a kind of machine, elaborately constructed beforehand and then left to itself to work out the principles implanted within it. If God stood to the universe as an inventor stands to a machine, this parallel might help us. But such a deistic view of God's relation to the world is no longer possible to us. For us no part of Nature down to its minutest atom is withdrawn from the ever-present energy of the indwelling God. What we call the laws of Nature are but the expression of His will, and all the forces that bewilder us with their complexity, awe us with their sublimity, or crush us with their might are forces which are wholly dependent on His omnipotent power. But when we have said this we perhaps have the clue in our hands that will help us to solve our riddle. Nature is the expression of a living will, and the majestic order which it presents to us speaks in eloquent language of the wisdom of that Being on whom it depends. At first sight this thought seems to negative the possibility of miracles. The deviation from order into the abnormal seems to suggest that the universe has broken down in God's hands, that a demand has been made upon it which it is not adequate to fulfil, and hence that it has been necessary to supplement it by recourse to extraordinary means. Moreover, our own age is far more inclined to emphasise the presence and activity of God in the common course of things than in what is unusual. And there is much to be said for this. It is not healthy for us to be seeking after a sign or to imagine that only what is marvellous can be Divine. Yet we must beware of the superstition of limiting God to the tracks along which His energy normally moves, and believing that no end, however worthy, and no emergency, however desperate, could induce Him to forsake the beaten path. We have no hesitation in making our personal impact on Nature felt in ways hitherto untried, and why should God, who exquisitely adjusts His means to His ends, be forbidden to manipulate freely that Nature which is but the plastic impression of His will?

Certain principles may be stated in order to mitigate our antecedent objection. We should, perhaps, be inclined to view a miracle with less incredulity if it was in a line with the working of forces already familiar to us. The accounts of Christ's works of healing, for example, are accepted by many who would deny that they were miracles. But the principle has a further extension. Where a miracle accelerates a natural process, or crowds a long development into a single moment, we feel that this, while strictly a miracle, flows in the same direction as the general stream of forces. If, again, there is a higher end to be gained, this must be taken into account in estimating credibility. The interests of spirit are supreme, and may constitute a worthy cause for the miraculous manipulation of matter. In the highest of all regions, that of religion, where it is a question of the revelation of God and the redemption of man, we must admit that the interests at stake warranted action of this kind on God's part, always provided that this was the fittest method of securing it. And we are, surely, not competent to judge whether this or another method would have been the fitter. God's action has so often been quite other than we should have expected, that we should be modest in deciding what is appropriate for Him to do. But we can see some reasons why this method should have been chosen. If a new revelation was to be given to mankind, miracles had their place in calling attention to it, and giving it a foothold in the world. They were its credentials till it could be accepted for its own sake. From this point of view they are a condescension to our weakness, ceasing when the need for them had passed. Further, they for the most part displayed the love and compassion of Jesus, in healing the sick and raising from the dead, in feeding the multitude and casting out demons. These were worthy ends in themselves. But one of the most important functions of the Gospel miracles is that they are signs of spiritual truth. There is an inner significance in them. If Christ feeds the five thousand, this is a symbol of the great fact that He is the world's bread of life. If the fig-tree withers at His word, it is a parable of the doom that awaits hollow profession, and especially of the doom of the

Jewish people. His healing of disease and raising of the dead show Him as the Lord of life and Victor of death, and are the pledge of the final conquest of all evil. And therefore the miracles are not mere prodigies, mere displays of power for the sake of display. They are witnesses to Christ's claims, proofs of His deep compassion, symbols of great spiritual realities. In all this there is nothing unworthy of God, unless we conceive of God as a rigorous pedant, iron-bound in adherence to a particular course of action. I believe, on the other hand, that God is not self-fettered, as many imagine, by what we call Natural Law. If to secure a higher end the laws of the lower realm need to be set aside, it is hard to see why we should feel an insuperable objection to God's doing so. We suit our means to our ends, and why should not He?

In the next place, we have to remember that the form which the revelation assumed was, to a certain extent, conditioned by the age into which it came. It is quite possible that had the Gospel come into a civilisation like our own it might very well have come in a completely different guise, and the element of miracle might have been far less prominent, since it would have been less suited to the intellectual temper of our time. We can also believe that the Gospel miracles are often prophetic of something which may yet be normal, the manifestation of forces at present held in check for reasons that we cannot wholly fathom, but which are ultimately to be released.

They are, in that case, not violations of law, but due to the emergence in experience of higher and hitherto unknown laws. They may be hints of some higher order towards which we are moving or which borders on our own.

So far, then, I have been pleading for a franker recognition of our limitations in the estimate of possibilities, and trying to dispel some of the antecedent objections to miracles. What has been said has not been intended to prove that the Gospel miracles actually took place. It has been meant to place the reader at a point of view where he may be able to divest himself of prejudice and enter on a dispassionate historical inquiry. When we come to discuss the question whether the miracles actually occurred, there are several points which deserve consideration. I call attention first to the intimate connexion between the miraculous and non-miraculous elements in the Gospels. It would be no easy task to cut out the miraculous and leave the other elements intact. They form the starting-point for much of the characteristic teaching, and sayings which only hypercriticism would regard as invented presuppose that miracles have taken place. And the analytic criticism of the narratives does not help us to discard the supernormal, for in the earliest stratum of Synoptic tradition this element is present.

In the next place, the miracles bear the stamp of sobriety and dignity. Those who are familiar with the products of unrestrained imagination pandering to love of the marvellous will be deeply struck by this quality in the Gospels. The comparison with the Apocryphal Gospels has in this respect often been made, and the repulsive, passionate, spiteful Jesus whom they set before us, performing grotesque miracles of ostentatious display, mere prodigies, devoid of all higher significance, designed to gratify his own desires, stands in striking contrast to the Jesus of the Gospels, who leads a quiet life of retirement till the time arrives for Him to undertake His mission for the world. In the Apocryphal Gospels Jesus strikes a boy dead for running against Him, turns clay sparrows into live birds, and performs many similar wonders. This literature shows how writers, who were not controlled by facts, imagined that a Being possessed of miraculous powers would act. If the Gospel miracles did not really occur, how is it that their narratives are free from the same glaring defects? If fancy had inspired them, would they not have told similar wonderful stories of Christ's boyhood? But they are true to the great principle that His miracles were only wrought for the sake of His mission, and therefore never till His ministry began. And along with the sobriety of the stories we may take tleir ethical character. Jesus does not work miracles for Himself. At the very outset of His career He refused to do it, and maintained that attitude steadfastly to the end. His miracles were, for the most part, deeds of compassionate love, revealing the depth of His tenderness and sympathy; they were of a piece with His whole character and life.

Again, we feel no disharmony in reading the Gospels between the miraculous and the other elements of the story. The writers move quite easily in every part, tell everything in the same matter-of-fact style, and sketch a character which leaves a firm and consistent impression. Their management of the supernatural would have been the precise point where they would have broken down if they had had no facts behind them. It is not easy even for a skilful writer to manipulate the supernatural, and fit it easily into a framework of ordinary incident. But we feel no sense of awkwardness or incongruity in passing from the normal to the abnormal in the Gospel narrative. Now the authors were not men of consummate literary genius, who by their unfailing literary tact secured this remarkable effect; they were plain and homely men, and their literary triumph was due to the fact that they faithfully recorded events which they would have had no skill to invent.

It may be urged that the Gospels arose in an unscientific age, when people were credulous about miracles and readily satisfied as to their authenticity. It is, of course, quite true that we are not dealing with scientifically-tested incidents, and quite possibly an observer trained in modern methods would have reported in different language from that used by our evangelists. But an examination of the narratives themselves shows us that miracles were not looked upon as a kind of everyday experience. The Gospels mention again and again the unbounded amazement that Christ's miracles excited. What struck the people was the uniqueness of His acts. They never saw it on this manner. Moreover, His enemies invented grotesque explanations of His miracles, just because they could not deny the facts themselves, and yet had to negative the inferences which were naturally drawn from them. The explanation of Christ's miracles given by the Pharisees, that they were wrought by Satanic power, shows by its very desperateness how urgently they felt the need of explaining facts too patent to be denied They may not have had the training of a modern scientist, but their eyes were sharpened by hate, and if they could have exposed a fraud or disillusioned a too credulous public they would have left no stone unturned to do so.

A theory which at one time had great vogue calls for mention at this point. Strauss argued in his famous *Life of Jesus* that the miracle stories were the outcome of a mythical tendency, and especially were influenced by the Messianic beliefs of the people and Old Testament narratives. Since His followers regarded Jesus as the Messiah, it was natural that the narratives of His life should represent Him as fulfilling the Messianic expectations, and thus, quite naturally and without fraudulent intention, the mythical stories grew up about Him. On Strauss's effort a few words may suffice. First, as Baur, who was his teacher and the famous founder of the Tübingen school, pointed out, Strauss attempted a criticism of the narratives without the indispensable preliminary of criticising the documents in which they are found. Secondly, the mythical theory took no account of the inexorable limits of time. Myths grow up far more slowly than Strauss realised. In the most important case of all, the Resurrection, we have evidence which carries us back to the very week of the death of Jesus, and Paul's evidence in general is sufficient to dispose of the theory as a serious interpretation of the career of Jesus. Lastly, it is just in the crucial cases that the theory turns out to be most unsatisfactory. On this I may quote the evidence of a sympathetic witness, who was himself a militant opponent of the belief in miracles. Pfleiderer, who contributed an introduction to the reissue of George Eliot's translation in 1892, has the following words : " Precisely the chief miracles—the birth of Jesus, His baptism, transfiguration, resurrection, the change of water into wine at Cana, the stilling of the storm, and walking on the sea—violence must be used to explain these miracles by reference to Old Testament types, and the Jewish idea of the Messiah offers no lines corresponding to these."

I would next call attention to other factors in the Gospel history which have to be taken into account in estimating the miraculous element. First of all, the Christian Church believes in the sinlessness of Jesus. Naturally that is a point on which I shall have something to say later. But if for a moment we adopt without discussion this point of view, it will surely influence our attitude not a little. In the first place, sinlessness is itself a moral miracle even more wonderful than the manipulation of matter implied in the physical miracles. Secondly, it was possible for powers to be entrusted to Him which could not have been safely committed to any one less good than He was. History is full of examples of men demoralised by the possession of despotic power. We think of Nero as a typical though somewhat extreme instance. But even the irresponsible tyrant who is fettered by no restriction of constitutional authority must recognise the limits imposed on humanity which even the most exalted may not pass. The savage chief who holds the life of his people in the hollow of his hand, the slave-owner who may practise unrestrained the most loathsome outrages and the most fiendish tortures on the hapless victims of his passions and cruelty, are instances which show us how dangerous it may be to delegate power to those who are so easily demoralised by it. But how much more terrible the power might be if the faculties thus entrusted were of what we should call a superhuman order. He who would fitly exercise these must be free from the faintest trace of self-seeking, and endowed with a

Divine holiness and beneficence. I do not say that this proves in any way that the miracles really happened, but I am pointing out the harmony of the character of Jesus with the works which are assigned to Him—they support each other.

Another feature in the Gospel miracles that deserves attention is the spiritual significance which attaches to many of them. This is especially the case with the miracles in the fourth Gospel. The author speaks of them as signs—that is, they are enacted parables which are not mere portents, but have a deep spiritual significance. The Feeding of the Five Thousand forms a text for a discourse on Jesus as the Bread of Life, the Healing of the Blind Man is a visible spiritual symbol of sight given to those who are inwardly blind. The miracles are thus not mere wonders, but they disclose in vivid concrete form some of the laws of the Kingdom of God. In this respect, too, the Gospel miracles are distinguished from many other narratives of the kind.

Lastly, let us remember the place of Jesus in universal history. The most important fact in human life and history is religion, whether we have regard to its intrinsic value or the part it has played in the affairs of men. Wherever we look in the long history of our race we find religion pre-eminent; it is that which strikes deepest into life. And by common consent of those best fitted to judge, Jesus stands in the history of religion without a peer. In Him centre the streams that flow out of the past, from Him have come those influences which have shaped and will shape the history since His day. And in a personality and an epoch so critical, so fraught with destiny, is it so incredible that strange and unknown powers should have been at work, that His beneficent energy might be released and achieve for humanity what might otherwise have been unattained? Horace, in a famous passage, warned the tragedian that he should not bring a god upon the stage unless there were an entanglement whose solution was worthy of a god. So, too, we may vindicate the place of miracle. The task to be achieved was of such vital moment, and sin had brought the coil in which humanity was ensnared into such a tangle, that for its unravelling we may well believe God would not shrink from bringing abnormal forces into play. I have little faith that a non-miraculous Christianity will be found to stand the test either of criticism or experience. It will have to be more or less. But our attitude to the Gospel miracles in general is naturally influenced to no small degree by our decision on the crucial problem of the Resurrection. I therefore propose to devote a special chapter to its investigation; but before I approach this I must discuss the question of the Supernatural Birth, which is at the present time exciting much interest.

CHAPTER XI

THE SUPERNATURAL BIRTH OF JESUS

IT is undeniable that for some time now the minds of many Christians have been much exercised on the question of the supernatural birth of Jesus. I wish, therefore, to say at the outset that I do not regard this question as one which vitally affects the Christian faith. It is important to emphasise this, because many Christians, very injudiciously as I believe, speak as if the Divinity of Christ and His sinlessness were vitally bound up with the question of His human origin. I desire, therefore, to express as emphatically as I can my belief that the Divinity of Christ is completely independent of the precise method by which He came into the world; and, secondly, to point out how dangerous it is to stake the fundamental truth of our religion on a fact which in the nature of the case could be only very slightly attested. The levity which is often displayed by exponents of Christianity is responsible for not a little present-day scepticism.

I wish, in the next place, to express my own belief that the doctrine does not provide us with a strong guarantee for the sinlessness of Jesus or help to explain it. I have never been able to understand why the transmission of a sinful human nature could not have come just as well through one parent as through two. It is quite true that we are dealing here with factors of which we know little, but it can hardly be seriously contended that the elimination of one factor leaves us with a sinless origin unless we are prepared to accept the Romanist theory that the Virgin Mary was herself from the very outset cleansed from original sin. Most of my readers will, I imagine, admit that Mary constituted no exception to the universal sinfulness of the human race. Hence we cannot explain the sinlessness of Jesus by the supernatural birth. So far, however, as the idea rests on the thought that virginity is a purer state than marriage, that I can regard only as a disgusting asceticism which sets itself up to be wiser than the Creator. It does not follow, however, that because a belief is not fundamental it is therefore unimportant. The belief in question presents many points of interest and deserves very attentive consideration. If it is true, it can hardly be devoid of significance, though we may not be in a position to point out where that significance lies. Now those who believe that whatever is in the New Testament is to be accepted simply because it is there naturally raise no question with reference to this matter. But that is not the point of view of those for whom I am mainly writing. They wish the matter to be foreclosed by no theory of inspiration, but to receive impartial investigation, and I myself hold strongly that this is the only ultimately satisfactory method of treating the subject. We approach it, then, just as we should any other problem in history.

It ought to be frankly admitted at the outset that a very impressive case can be built up against the historical character of the birth stories. And since I think that nothing is to be gained by refusing to look facts in the face, and to hear the utmost that can be said on either side, I begin by stating the case against the truth of the narratives. We have, in the first place, to set the silence of much of the New Testament literature. Modern scholars are all but unanimous in the belief that the Gospel of Mark is our earliest Gospel, and was employed in our first and third Gospels. We have then to notice the fact that this Gospel betrays no knowledge of the supernatural birth. Indeed, the friends of Jesus, when they heard of the multitudes that were thronging to His ministry, went out to lay hands on Him under the impression that He had lost His reason, and His mother was associated with His brethren in this enterprise. Had she been aware of the supernatural origin of her Son, as the first and third Gospels represent, it is argued that she would not have attempted to restrain His activity or placed such a construction upon it.

But we have a witness earlier even than Mark, and that is the Apostle Paul. He, too, although his Epistles are full of Jesus, never alludes to the fact in question, though he asserts His Davidic descent. In view of Job xiv. 1, it would be impossible to lay stress upon Galatians iv. 4 as a tacit allusion on Paul's part to it, especially as in that passage Paul is emphasising the community in experience of Jesus with His fellows rather than His distinction from them. And what is true of Paul is true also of the Epistle to the Hebrews. The author alludes to the fact that Jesus sprang out of Judah as notorious. He lays much stress on the reality of the Incarnation and the participation of Jesus in the lot of His brethren. He even refers to the body of Jesus as prepared by God, but he nowhere alludes to the mode of His birth. And so with the rest of the New Testament literature. Outside the first two chapters of Matthew and Luke, and a bare reference in the introduction to Luke's genealogy, the New Testament is entirely silent.

And when we pass on to consider these chapters the difficulties thicken about us. It is extremely hard and perhaps impossible for us to reconcile them. They tell an entirely different set of incidents. Matthew narrates the hesitation of Joseph and its removal by a dream, the marriage of Joseph and Mary, the birth of Jesus in Bethlehem, the visit of the Wise Men, their interview with Herod and return to their own country by another road in consequence of a dream which warned them not to return to the King, Joseph's flight with mother and child into Egypt in consequence of a dream, the massacre of the babes at Bethlehem, the return of Joseph to Palestine, his fear to return to Judea on account of Archelaus, and his residence at Nazareth, in Galilee, in consequence of a dream. This narrative is marked by striking peculiarities. Joseph is very prominent throughout, and no fewer than five dreams occur in a narrative of thirty-one verses. The writer betrays no knowledge that Nazareth was the home of Joseph and Mary, but suggests that it was selected for their abode in consequence of a dream.

The narrative in Luke tells us of the story of Zacharias and Elizabeth, the appearance of Gabriel to Zacharias in the Temple and promise of the birth of John, the incredulity of Zacharias and his dumbness, the visit of Gabriel to Mary at Nazareth and the Annunciation, the visit of Mary to Elizabeth and the Magnificat, the birth of John and the Benedictus, the enrolment under Quirinius and consequent visit of Joseph and Mary to Bethlehem, the birth of Jesus, the appearance of the angels to the shepherds and their visit to the child, the naming of Jesus, His presentation in the Temple and the story of Simeon and Anna, and the return of Joseph and Mary with Jesus to Nazareth. Here Mary receives a prominence not accorded to her in the story of Matthew, and from the first she is regarded as resident in Nazareth, and the birth at Bethlehem is due to the accident of the census. These very different stories naturally make on many the impression that they are hopelessly inconsistent with each other.

Added to all these difficulties there is the ominous fact that the story of demi-gods who have sprung from the mating of divine and human parents has had a very wide diffusion among heathen peoples. It is therefore only what might be expected when we find a similar origin attributed to Jesus of Nazareth. The claim that He was the Son of God naturally clothed itself in a myth of this kind.

These, then, are the main objections which the story arouses in many minds. I proceed to consider their validity. I do not wish to disguise that the difficulties are really serious. They are felt by some who have no prejudice against miracles and firmly believe in the Resurrection of Christ. At the same time I cannot help feeling that the force of the objections is frequently overrated. The silence of the New Testament outside the first and third Gospels is of very trifling importance. The Gospel of Mark does not attempt to give us anything beyond the history of which the apostles were themselves witnesses and which formed the subject of their testimony. Peter lays down as the qualification for apostleship that the candidates should have companied with the apostles all the time that Jesus was with them, beginning from the baptism by John to the day that He was received up. Similarly in his speech to Cornelius, and in Paul's address at Antioch, the same limit is observed. The birth and earlier years of Jesus accordingly lie outside the scope of the apostolic testimony to His career, and Mark abides faithfully by the limits which it observed. And in the very nature of the case the matter was not one to be proclaimed from the house-tops, especially while the mother of Jesus was still alive. It is, in fact, a question whether it had been disclosed by Mary to any of the apostles for a long time after the death of Jesus. It does not follow that Mark was unaware of the story when he wrote his Gospel, though this is quite possible. Nor is it clear from Mark's narrative that Mary herself shared the opinion that Jesus was beside Himself.

The case of Paul is somewhat different. His Epistles were written for the most part to churches which he had himself founded, and they presuppose the teaching he had already given to the members. This, it is true, does not apply to the Epistle to the Romans, or that to the Colossians, but in both cases he was dealing with those who were instructed to some extent in the Christian faith. It is therefore possible that the story of the supernatural birth had been communicated to the recipients of his Epistles. At the same time, I am very dubious about this. There is no allusion to such teaching in the Epistles themselves. Moreover, I suspect that Paul would have felt it desirable, in dealing with Christians who came out of heathenism, not to divulge to them all at once a story which they would only too readily treat as on a par with the myths of the demi-gods. And it is by no means im-probable that if he ever learnt the story, it was only comparatively late in life. If the third Gospel was written by Luke, it is most likely that he learnt it when he was in Palestine during Paul's imprisonment at Cæsarea, and if he knew it we may assume that he would communicate it to Paul. There is, however, no essential advance in the doctrine of Christ's Person in the later Epistles from that which we find in the earlier. From the first Paul regarded Jesus as the pre-existent Son of God who had become man, and we have no reason to suppose that he would have regarded the mode of birth as vitally affecting the construction of his central doctrine.

The fourth Gospel presents us with rather more interesting problems in this connexion. At the time when it was written the author can hardly have been ignorant of the story. It is generally agreed that he was acquainted with the Gospel of Luke, so that his silence concerning it can hardly be due to ignorance. It might, of course, be argued that it was due to rejection of it, but there is no reason to suppose that he would feel it out of harmony with his own doctrine of the Incarnation of the Logos ; presumably he would consider it a not unfitting mode in which that Incarnation might take place. But, apart from this, it is by no means clear that he was silent. In the thirteenth verse of the first chapter there is a very ancient reading, " Who was born not of blood, nor of the flesh, nor of the will of man, but of God." The usually accepted text reads the plural instead of the singular, and the reference is in that case to the spiritual birth of those who believed on the Name of the Logos. But the other reading, as Resch was the first to show, has very strong attestation, and it is accepted by such scholars as Blass and Loisy. If it preserves the original text, we probably have here a definite statement of the supernatural birth.

We may say, however, with high probability that the evangelist alludes in vii. 42 to the birth at Bethlehem. He represents the multitude as disputing the Messianic character of Jesus, some making the objection that the Messiah could not come out of Galilee since He must be of the seed of David and spring out of Bethlehem. It is strange that some should have inferred from this that the author wished to negative the Davidic descent and the birth at Bethlehem, still more that he was ignorant of these facts. The Davidic origin, decades before the Gospel appeared, was a matter of notoriety in the Church, and Jesus was Himself regarded as the Son of David in His lifetime. And the author is content to let the objection go without a single word of refutation, just because he could so surely count on his readers supplying the refutation for themselves. Nor must we forget that it was in the Johannine school that the supernatural birth received such prominence. Ignatius insists very strongly upon it.

I pass on, then, to the stories in Matthew and Luke, and I begin with their discrepancies. It is quite true that it is very difficult to escape the impression that the stories do not easily dovetail into each other. There are several points, however, to be considered before we draw far-reaching inferences from this. We cannot forget that it is a quite common phenomenon in history to have very different accounts given of the same incident. Even eye-witnesses of an event often disagree as to minute details. There is, it is true, no absolute contradiction between the narratives, still we should infer from Matthew that the residence in Nazareth was an accident ; and, on the other hand, we should not imagine from the story in Luke that the flight into Egypt and the circumstances which led up to it had ever occurred. Yet even here we shall do well to bear certain things in mind. The differences are partly due to the patent fact that in one case Joseph's point of view is insisted upon, in the other case Mary's. It was the series of events in which Joseph was most prominent that naturally bulked most in his reminiscences. This may not account entirely for the selection of incidents, for it is also crossed by the evangelist's characteristic interest in proving the Messiahship of Jesus from the Old Testament, on which I shall have something to say later.

As to Luke's narrative, I may point out that it immediately follows a personal statement by the author in which he claims to have " accurately traced the course of all things from the first." Such a statement ought to be respectfully received, and while, no doubt, there are scholars who impugn Luke's accuracy, it may be said with some confidence that his credit as an historian has steadily risen. He had considerable opportunity for investigation while he was in Palestine. It is also noteworthy that, while he tells a story so different in many of its features from that of Matthew, he coincides in some very important points, namely, in the central fact of the supernatural birth itself, in the location of it at Bethlehem, in the time at which it took place—the reign of Herod, in the subsequent residence of Jesus in Nazareth. Now, in view of the difference between the two stories, it is clear that they are entirely independent, and therefore that we have two witnesses who agree in this series of coincidences. Why should the birth be placed in Bethlehem if, as we are constantly told, Jesus was really born in Nazareth? Had we simply the first Gospel to deal with, it would be plausible to say that the prophecy of Micah created it. In answer to the Jewish objection that, according to the prediction in Micah, the Messiah must be born in Bethlehem, the story grew up that He was born there, but, owing to circumstances, removed to Nazareth. But it is by no means easy to apply this explanation to Luke's narrative, for he was not dominated in the same way as the author of the first Gospel by the necessities of Messianic apologetic, and he accounts for the birth in Bethlehem by reference to the census of Quirinius. It is impossible to go into the well-known difficulties raised by this statement; but, while it cannot be said that Luke's accuracy has been established in this point, it has not been proved that he made a mistake.

It is, I believe, highly improbable that heathen influence should be invoked to account for the stories. The New Testament, on the whole, is singularly free from marks of heathen influence, and it is intrinsically unlikely that one of the lowest features of pagan mythology, the story of heroes of mingled divine and human parentage, should have been adopted by its writers. Such stories would have been most repulsive to a Jew; they would have been equally so to Jewish Christians, especially as applied to Him whom they worshipped as the Son of God. The birth stories both in Matthew and Luke, but especially in the latter, are in their whole structure and point of view Jewish throughout.

Yet they cannot easily be explained as Jewish Christian creations. The Jews exalted marriage, and not virginity; and therefore there was no temptation to invent such a story by way of commending the Messianic character of Jesus to the Jews. But it may be urged that this is inconsistent with the Jewish belief that the Messiah was to be born of a virgin. But was there such a belief? Possibly there may have been, though it would not be easy to prove it. It may be asked, What about Isaiah's prediction of the birth of Immanuel? On this I must content myself with stating results, referring for a discussion of the question to my article " Immanuel " in *The Dictionary of Christ and the Gospels*. Isaiah's prophecy of Immanuel, since it was intended to reassure Ahaz, who was in the throes of the war with Syria, could not have related to an event which was to occur seven hundred years later. The Hebrew term translated " virgin " does not properly bear that significance ; it simply means a young woman of marriageable age. The Septuagint rendered by a Greek word which meant " virgin." Matthew adopts the same translation, but owing to the fact that he could go back to the Hebrew for himself, and that he diverges to some extent from the Septuagint in his quotation, it is not certain that he is dependent on the Septuagint here. But may we not argue that the Septuagint translation gave rise to the story of the supernatural birth ? This is improbable. It is questionable if it would account for Luke's story. But, secondly, a study of Matthew's Messianic proof-texts also makes it unlikely. These texts are in some cases so remote from the incidents which they are supposed to predict that we can infer with certainty that the event suggested them, and that they did not create the story of the event. And the same is probably true here. The author starts from the fact of the supernatural birth and goes to the Old Testament for a text in which it is predicted. His story of Herod is corroborated by the known character of that king. He was like a savage tiger where his personal interests were touched, and the least suspicion of disloyalty or dread of a rival threw him into a paroxysm of insane fury which stopped at nothing.

I close with some general reflections. In the nature of the case evidence for the event must ultimately be reduced to the testimony of Mary and, to a certain degree, of Joseph, and this we have at best at second hand. In the next place, we cannot discuss the question in a vacuum. Were we treating the case of some ordinary man for whom this claim was put forward we might excusably put it aside on the ground of the intrinsic improbability of the event and the weakness of its attestation. But in this case we are speaking of one whom we regard as the Son of God, and whose earthly career closed with the still more stupendous miracle of the Resurrection. We are speaking of the central Figure of all History. Approaching the story along these lines, we may feel that in a person so supernatural the Virgin-birth was natural. Again, the obvious fact that the story lent itself to so much misconstruction would have acted as a severe check upon its rise and diffusion. Had the disciples felt that otherwise they could not guarantee the position they assigned to their Founder, they would undoubtedly have taken the risk of claiming for Him a supernatural birth. But this was not the case. His Davidic origin was recognised long before the mystery of His birth was breathed in the Church. His Resurrection attested His Divine dignity. Paul had from a quite early period proclaimed His Divinity independently of any theory as to the origin of His humanity. Under those circumstances the story of the birth was strategically vulnerable and dogmatically unnecessary. Its origin is most easily explained if it embodied a fact.

And the very character of the narratives pleads in their favour. Their exquisite reticence, their beauty and freshness, their purity, their complete freedom from any trace of morbid reflection or vulgar curiosity are characteristics the significance of which we rightly apprehend only when we compare them with the fictions of the Apocryphal Gospels. These narratives show us what human invention would do when it set itself to speculate on the sacred facts, and the difference between the story as it comes to us in the Evangelists, and as it comes to us soiled and depraved by the coarse touch of the later writers, is the difference between the reverent description of fact and the unclean imagination of fiction.

CHAPTER XII

THE RESURRECTION OF JESUS

IN passing from the question of the Birth of Jesus to that of His Resurrection we are in the fortunate position that here our evidence is very considerable in quantity and early in date. At the same time we labour under the difficulty that there are several real or apparent discrepancies. It is no concern of mine to deny the discrepancies or to explain them away. I am dealing with the question as an historical problem, and, while the discordance of our sources may be inconvenient for rigid theories of inspiration, it does not render the narratives valueless for purposes of historical inquiry. Quite the contrary. As I have already said, the historian is constantly confronted with irreconcilable accounts of the same event given by people who had good facilities for observation. He welcomes discrepancies, since through comparison of them he is sometimes able to work back to an earlier form of the story. And whatever lack of harmony there may be in the statement of details, there is harmony touching the central events.

Let us remind ourselves of the situation in which the disciples of Jesus were placed by the crucifixion of their Master. They had followed Him to Jerusalem and been gratified by the homage of the multitude. It is true that Jesus had spoken ominous words about His death by crucifixion. Yet His utterances seem to have struck upon their ears without entering their minds. Their faith in the Messianic triumph of Jesus left no room for foreboding. With the triumphal entry the hour of destiny seemed to have struck, and they awaited eagerly the signal for the unfurling of the standard. But in perplexing inactivity the golden moments slipped away, while the enthusiasm of the multitudes died down or changed to a sullen resentment. Then all at once the catastrophe was upon them; the arrest, the futile resistance, their flight, His condemnation by the religious leaders of the people, the accursed death at the hands of the representative of Rome. Betrayed by one of His followers, denied by another, abandoned by all, His Messianic claim scouted by the Sanhedrin, and mocked by the pagan's title over the Cross, He had known the deepest of all agony—the agony of desertion by God.

What must all this have meant to His disciples? That He was disowned by the ecclesiastics need not have shaken them, for conflict with them had been a familiar feature of His ministry. That Pilate should have sent Him to His death, that might have seemed only too much of a piece with the brutal treatment which prophets had received from the world. But

o

that He had been permitted to die seemed to negative all their expectations for Him. They had looked to Him for the emancipation of Israel from Rome, and Rome had put an end to Him. Were He only a prophet, that could have been understood, but they had thought of Him as the Messiah, and His death seemed to contradict such a claim. Nor was this the deepest note in the tragedy, for He had died on the Cross, He had been hanged upon a tree. It is the comfort of the innocent, when fate goes against them, that they may appeal to the future from the present, and may commit their vindication to the care of God. But here it seemed as though God had endorsed the verdict of Caiaphas and Pilate, and by permitting Jesus to die on the Cross had placed upon Him the stigma of His own curse. For the Law had said, " Cursed is everyone that hangeth upon a tree," and to the pious Jew the curse of the Law was God's verdict, from which there could be no appeal. Who were they, weak, fallible mortals, to let their memories of the Master, the impression He had made upon them by the purity and beauty of His life, by the spell of His personality, the power of His teaching, the wonder of His works, stand for one moment against the unmistakable sentence of God ? What was there for them to do but, with their ideals shattered, to forget their misguided enthusiasm and return to the nets they had abandoned in obedience to His call ? Had His career ended with death, His cause would have perished with Him or the Cross, and been buried irretrievably with Him in His tomb.

And yet we know that they were not mastered by their despair, that they did not accept the Cross as God's last word upon Jesus, but that in the very city where their Lord had been crucified they proclaimed Him as Messiah, and boldly charged His judges with the guilt of His murder. What had happened to change these nervous Galileans, who, when the arrest came, saved themselves by flight, and left their Master to His fate? What cause had been at work to assure them that in proclaiming the crucified Messiah they were not fighting against God, but had Him on their side? For effects so remarkable we need an adequate cause. What that cause was they themselves did not doubt. Jesus had been crucified, but that was not the end of Him. He could not be held by the bands of death, but God had brought Him back from the tomb, and in so doing had lifted from Him the stigma of the Cross. Apart from such a conviction, it lies in the nature of the case that the Gospel of Jesus would have had no future. Christianity is built on the conviction of the disciples that Jesus who was crucified had risen from the dead and was seated in glory at the Father's right hand. It was in virtue of this unwavering conviction that the future career of Christianity became possible. We may look back now at the Gospel history and feel that, quite independently of the empty grave, the life and teaching of Jesus, culminating in His death, convince us of His greatness and divinity. But, humanly speaking, I do not see how we should ever have come to hear of Jesus at all apart from the disciples' belief in the Resurrection. The great thinkers of Greece looked forward to the immortality of the disembodied spirit. The Jews, however, could understand no such ideal as that; for them body and spirit constituted the human personality, and they would not have assented to the saying, "I am a spirit and have a body." A disembodied Jesus would have seemed to them a maimed Jesus, lacking an essential element of His personality. Had Jesus appeared in Greece, the Resurrection would not have been so necessary from the evidential point of view. There are many to-day who adopt an attitude similar to that which was natural to Greeks. They do not believe in a physical resurrection—that is a mere husk for the kernel, which is, that Jesus lives and reigns. And certainly this is the all-important thing, that Jesus is not a dead, but a living Christ. But the denial of an actual resurrection does not agree with the representation in the Gospels, nor, in my judgment, with that of Paul.

But for us, of course, the question is not as to the belief; that is practically admitted on all hands. The question for us is whether the belief was true or false. And we must deal with this question as a problem in history rather than in theology in the first instance. Our question is not one to be settled by appeal to writings whose narratives we accept because we treat them as inspired, but to documents we must treat as we would any other documents. It is a commonplace of critical method that great weight should be attached to contemporary documents and to documents of whose date and authorship we can be sure. It is natural, therefore, that we should begin with the testimony of Paul.

And in doing so it is well to remind ourselves of Paul's exceptional opportunities for investigation of the facts. He had been one of the bitterest opponents of the Christians. This was not because he misunderstood the Gospel, but because he understood it so well. With his penetrating insight he had very clearly perceived the drift of the Nazarene movement. He saw that logically it involved the setting aside of the Law and the consequent loss by the Jew of his most precious religious privileges, and therefore he flung himself with ardour into the work of persecution just because he realised the danger of this new doctrine. It would be inconsistent with all that we know of his subsequent career to suppose that he plied the Christians with no higher arguments than brute force. A trained dialectician, the master of a keen and relentless logic, deeply versed in the Scriptures, conscious of tendencies in the new religion which none of its adherents had realised, we may be sure that he appealed to violence only when argument had failed. And thus the Christian point of view became familiar to him, the story of the Resurrection standing in the first place. Those who had brought Jesus to His death were his intimate friends. The secret history of the trial was open to him ; he could learn, as the Christians could not learn, the official version of those tragic hours. Yet in spite of his initial horror at the blasphemous doctrine that a crucified claimant to Messiahship, notwithstanding the curse of God's Law, was God's Messiah none the less, in spite of the bitterly distasteful consequences involved in the acceptance of Him, in spite of the contemptuous rejection of Jesus by the leaders of the people, in spite of the wildly improbable story which the Christians told, in spite, finally, of the ruin of the great career which lay before him, Paul became a convinced follower of Jesus. He had been changed by what he took to be an appearance of the risen Jesus as he was on the way to Damascus, which in a moment revolutionised his point of view, and filled him with an overpowering conviction of His resurrection, never to be shaken by one moment's doubt.

But he learnt to know the case from the inside. He had met the chief leaders—Peter, with whom he stayed for a fortnight, and James, the Lord's brother. This he tell us in the Epistle to the Galatians, which is, fortunately, one of those Epistles accepted with practical unanimity by New Testament scholars. The reference to the fact of the Resurrection occurs many times in his Epistles, but it is only in 1 Corinthians xv.

that he gives a list of appearances of the risen Jesus. He says that He appeared to Peter, to His brother James, to all the apostles, and to five hundred brethren at once. Of these five hundred he asserts that more than half were still alive at the time he wrote. He tells us, further, that this Resurrection took place on the third day. He also insists that this fact of the Resurrection is one of the fundamental truths preached both by the apostles and by himself. Although this Epistle was written perhaps a quarter of a century after the death of Christ, it carries back the evidence much further. Paul had spent a fortnight with Peter three years after his conversion, and was therefore fully acquainted with his testimony. We are warranted, then, in accepting Paul's statement—so far as this, at any rate—that almost immediately after the death of Jesus, Peter and others, to the number of five hundred, believed that they had seen the risen Jesus. We owe this list to the fact that in the restless intellectual atmosphere of Corinth there had been disputes about the Resurrection. Otherwise we should have been without this invaluable piece of evidence. It is our earliest documentary attestation to the fact of the Resurrection, and therefore critics rightly make much of it. Yet it must be employed with certain cautions in mind.

First, it is only a bare list without details. This is due to the fact that Paul is not communicating fresh information to his readers, but reminding them of

information he had already given them when he
founded the Church. Secondly, it is not necessary
to assume that the list of appearances is exhaustive.
Paul chooses those which were best suited to his purpose. It was therefore natural that he should omit
the appearance to the women and lay stress on the
appearances to those who were, so to speak, the official
witnesses of the Resurrection. Thirdly, we must not
infer from the absence of detail that Paul knew of
nothing but appearances ; in other words, we must
not argue that Paul's sole ground for believing in the
Resurrection was the fact that apparitions of the
risen Jesus had been seen by His disciples.

It is now practically agreed that shortly after Christ's
death the apostles had reached the conviction that
their Master was alive again. Those who refuse to
admit that a physical resurrection had actually taken
place generally explain the belief as due to visions
which were not objective realities, but illusions of the
disciples, and contagious illusions. Most of these
scholars believe that the appearances of Jesus took
place in Galilee. It was there amid the familiar scenes
that the disciples recovered from their shock, and the
memory of Jesus cast once more its enchantment over
their minds. Faith revived and created for Peter the
vision of his Master. His enthusiasm proved contagious, and the vision was seen by one after another,
singly or in groups, and in one instance by more than
five hundred at once. This is the most hopeful line

for those to take who reject the physical resurrection. Yet it is open to the most serious objections, and has, indeed, been submitted to vigorous criticism by some who do not accept the fact of the Resurrection. Psychological illusions of this kind usually imply a condition of expectancy. But the Gospel shows us the disciples plunged in despondency, and quite incredulous when the news of the Resurrection was announced to them. If it be said that reflection on the life of Jesus created a reaction in which they attained assurance that the Cross could not be the end of Him, I must urge against this the shortness of the interval. Weizsäcker emphasises very strongly that, as Paul is our oldest source, we must be guided by his account in our reconstruction of the events. Accordingly he holds that the first appearance was to Peter. But he sees quite clearly that visions could not have been conjured up by the third day; and what adds to the difficulty is the hypothesis now received by several of that school, that the visions took place in Galilee. If the disciples, as some suppose, fled on the arrest of Jesus, they would not know whether He had died; if they fled to Galilee, after His death, as Weizsäcker thinks, they could have had no visions there so soon. But the point which needs attention is that the attempt to lengthen the interval is quite illegitimate. It is Paul himself who tells us that the apostles proclaimed that Christ rose on the third day. Now there are two points of great importance to notice here. The first is that Paul insists on the Resurrection as distinct from the appearances of Christ. Weizsäcker urges that Paul says nothing of what happened at the grave, to prove that he knew nothing of it. It is, of course, true that he gives no account, as do the Gospels, of appearances at the grave. But the Resurrection itself is a concrete fact for him. And what he meant by the Resurrection is clear. It immediately follows the mention of the burial, and therefore must be explained as a resurrection of the physical body; and in another place he defines it as a "quickening of the mortal body." But this can only mean that the earliest apostolic tradition knew not only of appearances, but of a resurrection of the body.

Further, we may well ask, What would have been the point of a reference to the burial of Jesus if the body that was buried played no part in the Resurrection? If Paul's faith rested simply on appearances of Jesus, the body need have played no part, and resurrection would simply have meant a manifestation of the spirit of Jesus from heaven. But when we remember that for Paul resurrection meant a quickening of the mortal body, and when we read that Christ was buried and rose again the third day, we are not at liberty to interpret him as meaning anything else than that the body, which was placed in the tomb dead, was quickened into life, quitted the grave, and appeared to the disciples. On the other interpretation Paul need have said no more than that Jesus died and on the third day appeared to the disciples. But in a summary statement of this kind we are not entitled to treat the burial as irrelevant and the Resurrection as identical with the appearances ; each of the four points—death, burial, resurrection, appearance—was vital to his case. And therefore we may conclude that Paul himself had no doubt that the death and burial of Jesus were followed by the resurrection of the body and the leaving of the tomb.

I pass on to another point which emerges from Paul's statement. Paul asserts that Jesus was raised the third day. Let us remember that we are dealing with the evidence of a contemporary of Jesus who speaks after he has familiarised himself with the case for the Resurrection and against it, that he speaks while many of the original witnesses are still alive, including the greater part of five hundred disciples to whom Jesus appeared at one time. Let us also remember that the majority of those who disbelieve in the Resurrection allow that we must treat Paul as our primary witness and prefer him to the rest. If there is one detail in the narrative that may legitimately be pressed, it is this chronological note. On the basis of Paul's account Weizsäcker asserts that the first appearance was to Peter, which Paul does not say ; while he denies that anything happened on the third day, which Paul very definitely affirms. It is hardly critical to play fast and loose with chosen authorities in this way. If Paul's testimony proves anything, it proves that the disciples believed that the physical resurrection of Jesus from the grave had taken place on the third day.

A further serious difficulty which may be urged against the vision hypothesis is the number of those who saw what they believed to be the risen Christ. Leaving aside all the Gospel narratives, and confining ourselves to Paul, we have his statement that Christ appeared to more than five hundred at once, and that the majority of these were still living at the time he wrote. It is not possible for us to question this testimony, for Paul uses it as evidence against those who doubted the Resurrection, and could have discredited it if untrue. We are therefore left with the stupendous difficulty of a subjective illusion of vision affecting five hundred people at once.

Another difficulty is that the visions cover a brief period only. This would be natural if the disciples had not been preoccupied with the thought of Christ. When our friends die, our thoughts naturally turn much to them for a brief period after their death. But gradually the vivid impressions fade, and other duties command our interest. If it had been so with the disciples' thoughts of Jesus, the fact that the visions soon ceased could be easily accounted for. But He was the central object of their thought and love. Their ardent hope was concentrated on the expectation of His return. It was precisely the state of mind from which visions might have been anticipated. Yet there are none. What does this prove, except that the early Christians were not the deluded enthusiasts that some believe them to be, and therefore that the brief period over which the appearances extend guarantees their genuineness?

Nor are these the only difficulties. If the body did not rise, what became of it? We have good grounds for believing that the grave was empty. No doubt if the visions took place in Galilee, at some considerable interval after the death, our grounds for believing this would not be so strong. But I have already shown that Paul's statement as to the third day must be accepted as decisive, and, if so, the visions cannot be placed in Galilee, for which a longer interval is required. We must therefore assume that they took place in Jerusalem. But, if so, it is not credible that the apostles should have omitted to make sure of the Resurrection by actual visit to the grave. They could hardly have faced the authorities with such confidence if they had not known that the grave was empty. The narratives have every probability on their side in their emphasis on the reluctance of the disciples to accept the evidence. This reluctance did not, in the eyes of the evangelists, reflect any credit on them, and they would have had no temptation to invent it. We may be glad of it, however, for it shows that the proof had to be forced upon them. The empty grave does not disprove the vision theory, but, taken with the other difficulties, it may fairly be said to do so.

The only other theory put forward by those who reject the physical resurrection which calls for discussion is that there really were no visions at all. This view, of which the late Dr. William Mackintosh was one of the ablest supporters, rests on the assumption that the language of the disciples was misunderstood. They meant no more than that Jesus still lived, not in the physical body, but in spiritual presence. It was reflection on the life and words of Jesus which convinced them that He could not have passed from them. He still lived and still worked. Death had not conquered Him, it had but changed the conditions of His life. One of them boldly seized this great conviction, and communicated his own glowing enthusiasm to others. The most obvious criticism to pass on this is that if they had meant this, it is strange that they should have expressed something quite different. To a Jew resurrection meant the resurrection of the body. A still more serious objection is that Paul undoubtedly, as I have already pointed out, understood the apostles to mean this. It is quite out of the question to suppose that he misunderstood them, for his knowledge of the facts is too detailed, and so keen an intellect could not have left the central fact obscure. Since the apostles cannot have deceived him, they certainly believed that they had seen the risen Christ ; and if the vision hypothesis be discarded, we must believe that He really appeared. Further, this theory gives no satisfactory explanation of repeated appearances to the same people. If the appearance to Peter means simply that Peter attained the conviction of Jesus' continued life, what interpretation must be placed on His appearance to him among the eleven, and again among those whom Paul styles " all the apostles " ? Did he attain this conviction on three separate occasions ? Such oscillation of belief certainly never occurred.

There is another view which is much nearer the original position. This is that the appearances were not hallucinations, but were merely spiritual in character, and that the body of Jesus was not reanimated. This position could be held with the admission of the empty grave, and, inasmuch as none of our canonical sources represent the disciples as witnessing the Resurrection itself, it might be accommodated not, indeed, to Paul's view of what happened, but to the historical inferences we are entitled to draw from his language. Nevertheless it is exposed to difficulties. In the first place, the Gospels do represent the body as subjected to physical tests. Secondly, we have to find some plausible explanation for the absence of the body from the tomb. It is, of course, quite easy to invent explanations with a little ingenuity. But have we gained very much by doing so in the way of making the event more in harmony with commonplace experience ? The combination of the appearances of what was taken to be the body with the absence of the body from the tomb is a coincidence so striking that, if we are willing to admit the possibility of the event, the Gospel statement of it provides the most natural explanation.

And do not let us forget that we are dealing with the most crucial event in history. It is not with a light heart that we can plead for incidents so abnormal, but yet we may undertake the task with a due sense of its seriousness when we remember of whom it is we are speaking, and all that He has meant for the world. It may seem easier at first sight to brush the whole story away as the merest folly. But when that has been done the task of unbelief is only beginning. For it must explain Jesus, it must explain Christianity, it must account for all its marvellous triumphs ; and till it has succeeded in doing so we may still repose our trust in Him who was dead and is alive for evermore.

CHAPTER XIII

THE DIVINITY OF CHRIST

I HAVE pointed out in an earlier chapter that the
Christian religion is distinguished by the position
it assigns to its Founder. While we claim that His
teaching surpasses in spiritual insight and power the
teaching of all other founders, yet we insist that the
supreme contribution He made to religion was not
what He said, but what He was and what He did.
And He is this to us in virtue of the intrinsic character
of His Person—He is the Incarnate Son of God, who
has become one with us in all things except our sin.
Before we inquire whether this claim for Him can be
justified let us think what it means. It means, first
of all, that in Jesus we have a revelation of the inmost nature of God. If Jesus is the Son of God, then
in His earthly life we have a translation of God's
moral and spiritual character out of the speech of
eternity into the speech of time. We no longer have
a mere description of God with all the inadequacy of
human language, but we are face to face with God
Himself living within the limits of our humanity His
own perfect life. In the next place, we have a pledge
of God's love. For if the doctrine of Christ's Divinity

P

is true, it means that for the sake of man God did not flinch from the uttermost sacrifice, but gave His own Son to be one with us in all our lot, shrinking from no excruciating extreme of misery. The Incarnation teaches us that God loves us better than He loves Himself.

But how are we to be assured that the doctrine is true? We must not be content to invoke external credentials, the miracles of Jesus which found their climax in the Resurrection. Not that these credentials are valueless. If on independent grounds we believe that the career of Jesus was marked by the exhibition of these strange powers culminating in the escape from the grip of death, we shall feel that these prepare us for a very extraordinary estimate of the character of His Personality. And if, on the other hand, we are convinced by our present line of inquiry that a strong case can be made out for His Divinity we shall find our conviction supported by the miracles. But the main stress of our proof must lie in the impression made upon us by Jesus Himself.

When we set out to prove the Divinity of Jesus it is well to understand precisely what we desire to prove. This will depend on our notion of what constitutes Divinity. It will not do to demonstrate that His career displayed the possession of omnipotence and omniscience. This might content those who had a merely pagan idea of God, but for ourselves this is impossible. Those who have sat at the feet of the world's great moral teachers, still more those who are familiar with Scripture, will insist that no being, however powerful and wise, can be God to us who does not exhibit the loftiest perfection of character. Accordingly, as we seek to prove the Divinity of Christ we must start with His character. Failure here is irretrievable. It can be redeemed by no success, however splendid, in other realms. I begin, then, with an attempt to show the sinlessness of Jesus. The task might at first sight seem hopeless. For, in the first place, the doctrine creates a prejudice against itself on the score of its antecedent improbability. Why *should* we make an exception in the case of Jesus, and believe that He was exempt from a failure, the reality of which we should assert in every other case ? Were we told, with reference to any other character in history, that he had been free from sin, we should refuse to believe it. Moreover, moral character eludes the closest observation, since it is only imperfectly revealed in deed and word. No one can fully enter into the recesses of the soul and read it in its naked reality. And if we cannot do this even with our most intimate friends, what chance have we of discovering the inmost character of one who lived nearly two thousand years ago, concerning whom we have very meagre information ? To the first of these objections it may be replied that our natural prejudice is no conclusive argument against the truth of the position. It justifies us in exposing it to exceptionally severe scrutiny, but in any case where sinlessness is alleged we have no right as scientific inquirers to excuse ourselves from the investigation on the ground of intrinsic improbability. The force of the second objection is real, but I hope the examination itself will show that we can reach a moral certainty along the lines of inquiry that I adopt.

I begin, then, with the impression which is made on ourselves by the presentation of the character in the Gospels. The best judges of human nature have united with the experts in saintliness in pronouncing the character one of unearthly purity, completeness, and perfection. I need not adduce quotations to prove this point, they are familiar enough. I am well aware that there are those who have discovered flaws in it, but I think I shall be doing them no injustice if I say that their criticism of Christ has been simply a demonstration of their incompetence for the task. The fact that a microscopic scrutiny has detected only such trivial blemishes might have prompted a modest doubt whether in a character otherwise so complete and stainless the blemishes were really there, or whether the discovery was not rather due to some obliquity in the critic's vision. But this general verdict forces on us the question, How did the evangelists come to depict a character of that kind? Even had they possessed a more exquisite delicacy, a more universal breadth of moral perception than seems probable, how were they to fashion a character which in all situations makes the same impression, and never betray it into a lapse from the loftiest standard? They were themselves sinful men, with their moral perceptions warped and distorted by sin. How could the stream have risen above its source? How could the sinful have imagined the sinless? And further, how, after they had imagined Him, could they have successfully conducted Him through so many scenes, set Him in conditions so varied, exposed to the play of forces so intricate, and yet have avoided all impression of artifice and charmed us by the simple realism of their narrative? Their success is due to the fact that they were drawing from real life, that the Figure of Jesus is a portrait, not a creation of imaginative genius.

But the existence of the portrait itself testifies to a conception of Jesus which was prevalent in the Christian Church. This was a conviction of His sinlessness. Even if we were to grant that none of the evangelists knew Jesus personally, which would be a very great concession, yet the material of their narrative was formed and current in the Church during the lifetime of the apostles. Hence we are confronted with the fact that a tradition, which ultimately goes back to themselves, which was formed in their own day and under their eyes, exhibited a sinless Jesus. We may infer that this was not without their own sanction. But not only have we a portrait in which sinlessness is implicit, we have the explicit claim made for Him by New Testament writers. It is made by Paul in letters composed before any of our Gospels were written. It is made in the First Epistle of Peter, in the Epistle to the Hebrews, in the First Epistle of John. It may, of course, be urged that many critics deny 1 Peter and 1 John to the apostles whose names they bear. At any rate, they testify to the impression which prevailed in the Church at the time when they were written. But it is not possible to dispose of Paul's evidence in so easy a way. If it be urged that Paul did not know Jesus, I reply that he knew the Christians who had known Him intimately, and he speaks of the sinlessness in a matter-of-fact way, which implies that he could take this estimate of Jesus for granted among his fellow-Christians. He never sets out to prove the sinlessness of Jesus, although with his tremendous conviction of the universality of sin he must have been alive to the obvious difficulties which the claim would present. Yet he never seems to imagine that any Christian will challenge it.

We may accordingly infer from these two lines of argument that the original apostles asserted the sinlessness of Jesus. It may be said, however, that this does not carry us so far as we wish to go, since their opinion was an inference from their observation of Jesus; but no observation could carry us behind the external facts and reveal to us the hidden springs of action. In reply to this, however, it must be said that their attitude towards Jesus involves something much more than this. For it included the impression made upon them of the estimate which Jesus formed of Himself. They could not have been in such familiar intercourse with Him without it coming to light, over and over again, that Jesus thought of Himself as sinful, if that had really been His inmost conviction. Jesus could not have allowed the impression of sinlessness to be created if He knew that it did not correspond with the facts. There must have been many occasions when Jesus' own consciousness of sinfulness, had He possessed it, must have forced itself into prominence. For the very conditions of His life with them made it imperative that He should speak to them in the most searching way about sin and penitence, not simply in outward manifestation, but in secret thought and disposition. How could He utter these penetrating words and yet always leave them with the impression that they had no application to Himself? We may therefore infer with confidence, from the apostles' conviction of His sinlessness, that it was a fact.

But we have a stronger line of evidence than the impression made on ourselves by the Gospel portrait, or the impression made on the apostles by their experience of Jesus, and that is the testimony of Jesus' own consciousness to His freedom from sin. It might be urged that no sinful fallible beings are ultimately in a position to decide upon this. I think, indeed, that we are led, by the two lines of evidence I have just presented, to a very high degree of probability. In my judgment, however, what definitely settles the question is the testimony of Jesus Himself. This is of various kinds, and in estimating its weight we must bear certain considerations in mind. In the first place, we have to remember that Jesus stands unrivalled as an ethical teacher. No one has so realised the fact of sin and its heinousness, read it in its subtlest forms with such sure and penetrating gaze, has recoiled with such horror and loathing from it, has realised its all-pervading presence, as He has done. There is no one who has more fervently condemned everything in the nature of hypocrisy, or whose sincerity we may more completely trust. Moreover, since it has often been observed that an advance in holiness brings with it a keener consciousness of imperfection, that the confessions of the holiest are those most filled with contrition, we may expect here, if anywhere, to have the keenest sense of moral failure and of unworthiness before God. But we find nothing of the kind. His only agony is for the sin of others, there is none for His own. He demanded penitence and was a foe to all self-righteousness, He would have shrunk with horror from any exaggerated claim for Himself, yet there was no tinge of remorse or repentance, no expression of His own need for forgiveness, no conviction of sin, no tragic note as He looked back on His career. His fight with temptation was more terrible than ours, yet His soul was not seamed with the scars of defeat. What does all this mean ? In the case of some it might mean an utter blindness of moral perception, or it might testify to a deep insincerity. But both of these are impossible in the case of Jesus; hence we cannot escape the conclusion that He believed Himself to be sinless, and was right in doing so.

And this conclusion is confirmed by other considerations. If there is one thing well attested in the records of His life, it is that He claimed to be the Judge of mankind. This claim in itself involved sinlessness. For how could a sinful man presume to judge his fellow-sinners ? I might add that it is a claim to be able to read the inmost secrets of men's hearts, for only one who possessed this faculty could pass a righteous judgment. It is a claim also to Divine wisdom which should enable Him not only to know the facts, but to take the right action upon them. And, lastly, it implies the Divine right to be the arbiter of men's destiny. Moreover, He claimed the power to forgive sins and actually did forgive them, and He believed that His death stood in a vital relation to the pardon of human sin. Now this would have been impossible in one who combined so keen a sense of the moral ideal with a consciousness of personal sinfulness on His own part. We may feel, then, that the evidence carries us far beyond the point that Jesus was a very good man or even the best of men. Between Him and us there is a deep gulf fixed ; in His sinlessness He stands with God, not with ourselves.

Now what explanation are we to give of this fact, which constitutes Him so strange an exception to the common lot? What is the secret of personality that lies behind the solitariness in character? We must, of course, beware of so interpreting the sinlessness of Jesus as to regard it as a pale negative quality. It is not the mere absence of defect, but positive perfection of character that we claim for Jesus. This is a moral miracle compared with which the physical miracles fall into a subordinate place. We are, therefore, forced to enter on other lines of investigation that shall solve for us the mystery of His being. The Church has expressed its conception of its Founder in the confession of Him as the incarnate Son of God. This is a loftier claim for Him than the claim of sinlessness, though it is necessary to demonstrate the sinlessness before we can accept the Divinity. Now, there are various arguments which converge upon the vindication of the Church's confession. We have the place which He fills in history, and especially in religion. There is the impression He made upon His followers, there is the claim which He made for Himself. It will be my duty to conduct the investigation along these lines.

I pass on, then, to consider the place which Jesus holds in history. He stands in a relation alike to the Past which lay behind and the Future which stretched before Him. The former we may summarise in the familiar term, "the preparation for Christ." Pre-eminently this preparation is associated with Israel, and that not in the form in which it was formerly presented. The old argument from prophecy threw its emphasis on details in Christ's life which, it said, had been predicted in the Old Testament. Now, it is not difficult to show that much which passed for proof will not bear the interpretation put on it. But, apart from this, such arguments do not in themselves appeal to the intellectual temper of our time. And it laboured under this general defect, that it could not, as we say, see the wood for the trees. The great prediction of Christ is the history and religion of Israel taken as a whole. In Him the long process attained its climax and achieved its goal. We see through the whole history God working by the principle of selection. One nation is chosen from all the nations of the earth, and out of it one tribe is chosen. And in that there is a remnant of those who looked for the Consolation of Israel, and out of the remnant the Messiah is born. The development led up to Christ, and found in Him its fit crown.

The people of Israel had been gradually trained by God's long self-revelation till it was possible for the final disclosure to be made. But what is true of the history of Israel has its counterpart in those of Greece and Rome. Greek culture and philosophy created a terminology and a mould into which the new truth might be cast, and by its own failure to realise its ideals, pointed to the need of some new power. For the world at the coming of Christ presented the mournful spectacle of moral collapse. The conquests of Alexander, followed by those of Rome, had created the field that the Gospel needed, bringing the larger part of the progressive peoples into one empire, and so breaking down national barriers as to prepare them for a universal religion. If Jesus came just at this propitious time, we have some reasons for believing that it was no mere chance that He came when He did. It would rather seem that there had been deliberate preparation for Him, that He had come in the fullness of time. In other words, God had Himself controlled the course of history that these converging lines might meet on Him.

And this argument is confirmed by that from the history of Christianity itself. It might be said, the success of Christianity is not so wonderful after all, for on your own showing the soil was ready for it. No doubt this does help to account for its rapid growth, but the fact that the soil was ready has to be explained. Yet, when everything has been said, the actual success of Christianity was of the most startling kind. A Galilean carpenter proclaims a new religion of the most exalted spirituality and morality. He achieves for a time great popularity, but is crucified by the Roman procurator at the instigation of the religious and political leaders of His own countrymen. A small band of disciples begins to preach that He has risen from the dead, and on this basis the new religion spreads, and in a very brief period penetrates every part of the Roman Empire, and the Galilean Peasant, who had a short time before been crucified, has won the allegiance of those who owe none to Cæsar. How was it that a religion which came out of the bosom of a people so despised and hated as the Jews, whose Founder had died a death counted accursed by the Jews, and which for all nations had a stigma resting on it far worse than with us attaches to the gallows, a religion attested by a story of a resurrection that must have seemed to the cultured Greek and Roman a wild absurdity fitly matching so stupendous a folly as the worship of a crucified Jew, how was it that such a religion thus made its way? Its lofty teaching ought to have won for it recognition, it may be said, yet the fact remains that Epictetus spoke of the Christians with cold disdain and Marcus Aurelius bitterly persecuted them. And to the populace such teaching appealed still less. To the common people the Christians were atheists. They would have been less unpopular had they had sacrifices in their worship or images, but they had none of these things. It was, moreover, incompatible with all other religions, so that Christians could not conform to many of the usages of social life, which involved a recognition of heathenism. Worse still, they could not sacrifice to the genius of the emperor, and were thus regarded as disloyal citizens. Meeting in secrecy, since it was dangerous to hold their assemblies otherwise, dark and shameful stories were widely circulated and easily believed. The religion did not come with the glamour of a hoary antiquity, nor was it a national religion, such as would have been permitted by Rome for political reasons. Without the prestige of wealth or learning, of social position or civil power, it permeated all ranks of society with a swiftness that seems almost incredible. And let it be remembered that it had its rivals. It was not the only new cult which competed with the old religions for popular favour. Why did the religion of Jesus conquer the empire, while Mithras and Isis and Serapis are barely known to the vast majority of mankind? Circumstances favoured them far more than they did Christianity. Was it not because Christianity was the word of the living God, which could not return to Him void?

And we have more than the early triumph of Christianity. It has formed one of the most important elements in the history of the last sixteen or seventeen centuries. No one can be other than amazed if he seeks to free his mind from the blunting influence of familiarity and asks himself what it means that so vast a phenomenon with such stupendous consequences has struck into the stream of human history. Every student of history is aware how enormous the influence of Christianity has been. I do not labour this point, but we must have some adequate cause for an effect so great. It will be worth while, however, to touch on an objection, to which I have already alluded and which might readily occur to the minds of some readers. It might be said, with some show of reason, that Christianity has worked for evil as well as for good. The cruelty, the ferocity, the mutual hatred of Christians, the horrors of the Inquisition, the fiendish atrocities connected with the conquest of America, the massacre of St. Bartholomew, the fires of Smithfield, the persecution of the Scottish Covenanters, it might be said, must be debited to the account if a fair balance is to be struck. And then the hostility which the Church has displayed to science, its frequent condonation or even active support of tyranny, its sacrifice of the poor to the rich, of the weak to the powerful, might also be urged against it. It is, indeed, the shame of Christians that these things should be so largely true.

But there are several considerations to be borne in mind. In the first place, Jesus Himself gives no warrant for conduct so reprehensible. His precept and practice alike condemn it. It is only a deep unfaithfulness to His teaching which is expressed in such things as these. Moreover, it has passed into a proverb that nothing is so bad as the corruption of what is best, and this in itself accounts for a large element in the indictment. The very excellence of Christianity is attested by the horrible character attached to its corrupt forms. But, apart from this, we need to discriminate. Life is a complex thing, and it is no simple matter to disentangle the threads. And it is very easy to urge as an objection to Christianity what really does not belong to it at all. Let us consider the historical situation. The Gospel came into the world as leaven; it was set originally in a Jewish, but quickly spread into a Gentile, environment. It was thus planted in a deeply corrupt paganism, bringing into it new ideas of pity and tenderness, of meekness and purity, of patient endurance and triumphant hope. It brought a loftier conception of God, of religion, and of morality. But it was natural that those who came under its influence should be imperfectly Christianised. The New Testament itself makes that plain. The spectacle of the Corinthian Church is very disenchanting. A more deep-seated corruption was for a long time kept at bay by the illegal status of Christianity which might at any time lead to persecution. When, however, Christianity became the religion of the empire streams of pagans entered the Church, in most cases, we need not doubt, with a real conviction that Christianity was true, but with the most imperfect sense of its claims upon them. Hence for many centuries the Christian Church was largely a baptized paganism, and although the pagan elements are being slowly eliminated we are very far as yet from that desirable consummation. Hence much that is put down to the account of the Gospel might be more truly charged against the paganism which, but for the immortal principle that lived within the Christian religion, would have quickly stifled it. And, lastly, we ought not to forget that it is the Gospel itself which has largely created the ethical standard by which we condemn the misdoings of the Church.

It is undeniable that it is the Christian spirit which has worked for the amelioration of human misery, has abolished slavery, softened the horrors of war, put an end to infanticide, reformed our prisons, built hospitals and orphanages. Its fundamental doctrine of the Fatherhood of God, with its corollary the brotherhood of man, gives us at once the impulse and the programme of social reform which even yet has been but poorly carried into effect. And were the story not so familiar, I might linger on the redemptive achievements of Christianity in the case of the individual. The Gospel is constantly working miracles of reformation, and there must be few of my readers who are not familiar with some cases where men of notorious character have been radically, and often instantaneously, transformed by the power of Christ. But, after all, the arguments from miracles, from the preparation for the Gospel, from the marvellous spread of Christianity, are largely of the nature of credentials. To say this is not to disparage them as worthless, but to put them in their proper place. The great argument for Christianity is Christ Himself.

Christ is, in the first place, the supreme Teacher of religion. His central doctrine was that God was the universal Father, and therefore that all men were brothers. He bade men love God and serve Him as children should love and serve their parents, and He encouraged them to trust to the uttermost their Father's love and care for them. Nay, He even commanded men to love their enemies and do good to those that persecuted them. His blessing rested on the pure in heart, the lowly, and the meek. He had an unfaltering belief in the infinite worth of each soul to God, and in the possibilities that were open to every man, even the worst. Yet He saw clearly and taught plainly that men were sinful, and needed to repent and turn to God. It is sometimes said, Everything that Jesus said had been said before Him by others. Let us grant that it is true, what then? Originality may or may not be a merit. If the truth has already been uttered, the merit lies in repeating it, and giving it new and fuller application. But there are other considerations to be borne in mind. We have no other teacher who so completely eliminated the trivial, the temporal, the false from his system, no one who selected just the eternal and the universal, and combined them in a teaching where all these great truths found their congenial home. These parallels from the teaching of others to that of Christ are brought together from this quarter and from that; how was it that none of these teachers furnishes us with any parallel to the teaching of Christ as a whole, while each of them gives us such truths as He expresses mingled with a mass of what is trivial and absurd? How was it that a carpenter, of no special training, ignorant of the culture and learning of the Greeks, born of a people whose great teachers were narrow, sour, intolerant, pedantic legalists, was the supreme religious Teacher the world has known, whose supremacy here makes Him the most important figure in the world's history ?

But it is a great mistake to speak of Him as if He were merely a teacher. For Christianity is not a mere moral philosophy, it is a moral and redeeming force. We needed more than a teacher, we wanted a Saviour. To have set before us the loftiest ideal would only have brought home to us more keenly our utter inability. But Christ is not only a teacher, He is a Redeemer. As such He has from the first been proclaimed by His followers.

And this brings me to consider the impression made by Jesus on the early Christians. The doctrine of the Divinity of Christ was soon formulated. We learn from Pliny's letter to Trajan, written early in the second century, that the Christians sang hymns to Christ as to a god, and the contemporary Christian writers contain much evidence to the same effect ; while it is undeniable that they considered themselves to maintain a belief in the unity of God. Naturally it was not easy to hold together with perfect balance and clearness the unity of God and the Divinity of Christ. Hence some of the early Fathers used language that to a later generation would have seemed dubious. But the New Testament presents us with a very lofty doctrine of Christ's Person.

19

I begin with the case of Paul. Take it how we will, the Conversion of Paul is in itself a striking testimony to the greatness of Jesus. Whatever attitude we may adopt to Paul's theology, no sound student of history can deny that he was one of the world's greatest men. He had everything to predispose him against Christianity. Assume the Christian doctrine to be true, and his conversion falls naturally into its place. But assume it to be untrue, and what must the force of that Personality have been which captured a man of Paul's magnitude and carried him His willing captive in His train? How, then, did Paul define the nature of Jesus? It is uncertain whether He actually applied the term "God" to Him, though in my judgment that is the truest interpretation of Romans ix. 5. But what he said of Him elsewhere can scarcely be satisfied by any doctrine short of His Divinity. He affirms His pre-existence, and assigns to Him the whole work of Creation, even of the loftiest angelic powers. He claims for Him that He existed originally in the form of God and was the image of the invisible God. He is the centre of cohesion which keeps the whole universe together. And some of Paul's indirect language is even more striking than the direct claim. We cannot accept the Authorised Version translation of Philippians ii. 6, "Thought it not robbery to be equal with God," and the exact sense of the passage is not easy to determine. Not improbably the meaning is that He counted not equality with God a thing to be clutched at. But of what creature could such a renunciation be adduced as an instance of humility for which Paul here quotes it? Humility is seen in waiving a claim which we have a right to make. It is no token of lowliness to refrain from aspiring to that which we have no title to possess. The passage is thus seen to be an even more striking expression of Paul's belief in Christ's essential Divinity than if the apostle had put the claim in the direct form given in the Authorised Version. I have by no means exhausted the evidence that Paul regarded Jesus as Divine, but this may perhaps suffice for my present purpose.

Substantially the same doctrine is to be found in the Epistle to the Hebrews and the Fourth Gospel. Both assert the Divine Sonship of Jesus, both assert that He existed before the worlds and was the agent in their creation. The former describes Him as the radiance of the Divine glory and the impress of God's essence, the clear-cut facsimile of His essential Being. The latter describes Him as the Logos who was in the beginning with God and was Himself Divine. Some of the other New Testament writings are less explicit, but if we carefully think out what is involved in their utterances about Jesus we shall see that they cannot be satisfied by anything but a high doctrine of His Person. It may be urged, however, that the doctrine was created by Paul, and that we can therefore attach no independent importance to its presence in the other New Testament writings, since their authors derived it from Paul. Now, I willingly admit that the Epistle to the Hebrews and the Fourth Gospel exhibit Paul's influence, and that therefore, so far as they are concerned, a plausible case might be made out for attributing the doctrine to this source. But it is proper to point out at this stage that other influences are traceable in these writings. The Jewish Platonism of Alexandria has exercised a profound influence on the author of the Epistle to the Hebrews, and has possibly affected the theology of the Fourth Gospel. I grant also that the First Epistle of Peter presents us with a substantially Pauline type of theology.

But there are very important considerations to be urged against the view that the doctrine originated with Paul. We have, first of all, a lofty doctrine of Christ's Person quite independently of Paul. It is generally recognised that we have a very primitive Christology in the speeches of Peter in the Acts. It is quite true that we have not here the fully developed doctrine which is found in the Pauline Epistles; but even here Jesus is regarded as a worker of miracles, as having been raised from the dead and exalted to the right hand of God. He is identified both with the Messianic King and with the Suffering Servant of Yahweh of whom we read in the Second Isaiah. He is described as the Holy and Righteous One, and the Prince of Life, in His name miracles are wrought and salvation is exclusively given, and through Him comes remission of sins. He is a Prince and a Saviour, and is ordained of God to be the Judge of quick and dead. It is He who pours out the gift of the Holy Spirit upon His followers. Here, therefore, is no trace of the Pauline teaching, yet when we put all these things together and estimate their total impression we can see that it was in order to do justice to what they implied that the doctrine of Christ's Divinity was formulated. The Book of the Revelation represents a different tendency from the Pauline. Yet its doctrine of Christ's Person is as exalted as Paul's. He is the First and the Last and the Living One. He is the Lamb who is associated with Him that sits upon the throne. He is King of Kings and Lord of Lords and the recipient of Divine honour. The significance of this lofty doctrine is all the more striking when we consider how intensely Jewish the Apocalypse is. And if it is really the work of John the son of Zebedee, as several scholars still believe, we can hardly overrate the importance of the fact that one who had been an intimate friend of the historical Jesus should hold so lofty a doctrine of His Person.

In the next place, the absence of the term "Son of Man" in the Pauline Epistles is a striking proof that they are not the primary sources of this doctrine. I do not enter here into the tangled problems touching this title which have called forth so many discussions during the last ten or fifteen years. We can reasonably account for the prevalence of the title in the Gospels and its all but complete absence from the rest of the New Testament only by the view that it was a title actually applied by Jesus to Himself. Whatever be the precise sense in which Jesus employed it, it assigns a unique dignity and meaning to His Person, and, as we shall see later, it is in the direction of Christ's teaching rather than of Paul's that we must look for the origin of the doctrine.

Once more, we have no trace of any opposition in the early Church to Paul's doctrine of the pre-existence or of the Divinity of Christ. We are all familiar with the conflict created in the Church by Paul's doctrine of the abolition of the Law. Now, fundamentally, Paul's doctrine that the Law was abolished rested on the estimate which he had formed of the work of Christ, and that rested in turn on the doctrine of His Person. For him it was impossible to give the work of the Son of God a place secondary to the Law. But, though logically the high doctrine of Christ's Person and the high doctrine of His work go together, the Jewish antagonists of Paul, while attacking one, did not challenge the other. Even if we consider that they may not have been alive to the logical inconsistency of their position, which is, of course, quite probable, it is clear that they did not realise any discord between Paul's view of Christ's Person and their own. The importance of this fact is that as rigorous Jews they would be naturally suspicious of any novel doctrine which seemed to impair the unity of God, and thus contradict the monotheism which was their deepest conviction. If, then, they did not attack Paul's doctrine here, it must have been because they were aware that this was no novelty, but a doctrine warranted by the teaching of Jesus Himself.

And, lastly, what should have led Paul to create the doctrine if it was a mere private speculation of his own? We must, in the first place, remember that Paul came to the subject as a trained Jewish theologian, and therefore as one whose fundamental doctrine was that of the unity of God. He shrank with horror from anything like polytheism. His instinct, therefore, would be to do nothing which might seem to imperil the belief in the Divine unity. In the next place, this was all the more important in view of the sphere of his labours. He was working in the Græco-Roman world, and its polytheism would have served as a constant warning to him of the danger that he might turn the Gospel into a new heathenism by setting Christ as a Divine figure by the side of God. Moreover, it is not clear that he might not have constructed his theology in such a way as to satisfy its necessities by some doctrine of Christ's Person short of His Divinity. For all of these reasons we may believe, on purely historical grounds, that Paul did not create this conception of Christ's Person, but received it from another source. Even at the point which we have reached it would be most natural to think of it as derived from the teaching of Christ Himself. But in order not to leave the matter one simply of inference, it will be my next duty to show that the doctrine was based on the teaching of Jesus Himself.

Accordingly I pass on to consider the testimony of Jesus to His own Divinity. That He laid claim to sinlessness we have already seen. That He believed Himself to be Divine I must now seek to show. That belief is attested by both direct and indirect evidence; there are utterances which assert it, there are utterances which imply it. If I could assume the authenticity of Christ's sayings in the Fourth Gospel, the claim would be made out, but in view of the widespread distrust of that Gospel I think that it will be wiser to rest my case on the presentation in the Synoptists. It is a singular proof of the veracity of these Gospels that, while they are later in time than the Pauline Epistles, they do not use the Pauline terms in their report of the references of Jesus to Himself, they are untouched for the most part by the later Christological development. And yet how stupendous are the claims which He makes for Himself in these Gospels.

I begin with a passage which cannot have been invented, since the disciples of Jesus would not have put into His mouth a confession of His ignorance. In Mark xiii. 32 we read, "But of that day or that hour knoweth no one, not even the angels in heaven, neither the Son, but the Father." The terms move upward in an ascending climax, and the Son, even in His humiliation, receives His place above the angels, while the use of the term itself implies a unique filial relation to God. We are not, then, surprised that He claims to be greater than Solomon and the temple, that if He is David's Son He is also David's Lord. The earlier messengers of God to Israel are the slaves of the owner of the vineyard, but He is the Son. He exercises the Divine prerogative to forgive sins, He claims to be the Judge of the world, and at the judgment He will send forth His angels to do His bidding. To Him all things have been delivered by the Father, and He asserts for Himself that He alone knows the Father and alone is able to reveal Him to others. He demands the utmost sacrifice, that men should subordinate to His claims the dearest ties of kinship and lose their lives for His sake. His blood institutes the New Covenant between God and man, He gives His life a ransom for many.

It may, indeed, be asked why Jesus practised so much reticence in making His claims. The reason lay in the historical conditions. In the first place, He did not wish to give His disciples the doctrine on His mere authority. It was far better that they themselves should reach the conviction from an unbiased consideration of the facts than that by a premature disclosure He should lead them to accept it on external authority. It was only after He had been with them and they had seen Him, not simply as the crowd saw Him, but in the familiar intercourse of the home, that He could propound the question as to the impression His Personality had made. And while the multitudes were convinced that there was something extraordinary in His Person, those who knew Him best had attained a higher conviction of its nature. But it was not necessary for Jesus simply to lead them to an unforced belief in His Divinity, but the Messianic ideas of His followers were at first so crude and unspiritual that the utmost caution was needed if He was not to set their thought on false lines.

It is not only the explicit assertion which has to be taken into account, we must consider also what is implied. His fundamental doctrine was the Fatherhood of God, and He Himself was truly man. Yet, in spite of His sense of kinship with His fellows, He does not speak of " our Father " as if the relation in which He stood to God was as their own ; He speaks of My Father and your Father, and if He uses the term " Our Father," it is when He is giving to His disciples a model form of prayer that they may use. He supersedes with His simple " I say unto you " even the Law. He needs no authority higher than His own. He is master of every situation, free from all embarrassment ; there is a sense of distance and distinction from us, a self-assertion of the loftiest type. There is about Him a universality, a freedom from the limits of race and sex and time which take Him out of the class of our ordinary humanity. What lies behind His occasional teaching is the serene and large knowledge of spiritual things, His lucid vision of God, His firm and easy command of the whole range of Divine truth. And what is very remarkable is His untroubled confidence in the future, His complete freedom from anxiety as to the progress of His Gospel. Consider only the fact that He wrote nothing. He anticipated a speedy end to His career. He knew the frailty of His followers, and yet He did not take what would seem to be the most ordinary precautions to secure that His teaching should be preserved. He uttered His matchless sayings in rich profusion, but He gave Himself no concern that they should be written down and thus saved from the failure of memory or other accidents which time and chance might bring. Partly this was due to the fact that Christianity was not to be a new law, but a new spirit; but it also testifies to the Divine confidence He had in the impression made by His Person, which He rated even more highly than His teaching. And yet even of this word, secondary though it was to His Person, He could say with calm conviction, "Heaven and earth shall pass away, but My word shall not pass away." Were we to be told of some historical person that he made claims for himself, direct or indirect, such as those made by Jesus, we should feel that we were probably dealing either with a conscious impostor or with a victim of megalomania. But no sound historical student would assert this of Jesus. His absolute sincerity rings through all He said and did. It was finally proved by the fate which He would not escape by retracting a claim that His judges regarded as blasphemy. And what but utter incompetence could utter the charge of insanity against One who impresses readers of the Gospels by the breadth and the balance of His views? He was no deluded enthusiast, for such a man could never have been the great Teacher who founded the highest and purest religion the world has known. Could the best of mankind have yielded their glad allegiance to an amiable but deluded fanatic? Jesus, indeed, combined qualities which at first seem to be irreconcilable, a stupendous self-assertion and affirmation of regal authority with a meekness and humility and an utter freedom from arrogance. It is in the same breath that He claims a unique relation to God and says that He is meek and lowly in heart. If, then, I hold the doctrine of the Divinity of Christ, it is primarily because I believe that He Himself claimed to be the Son of God, and His self-testimony is worthy of all acceptance.

And now I return to develop an argument I have already mentioned in this chapter, that I may point out how the claim of Jesus is corroborated by another set of considerations. No one could consider the history of Christianity without being impressed by the amazing slenderness of the apparatus compared with the stupendous character of the result. Nothing

could be more fantastic than the story of Jesus and
His achievement viewed as a natural human development. All the conditions were against Him if we have
regard to what impresses mankind and leads to the
attainment of success.

First of all, there was His country. It was a tiny
land, and, although not so isolated as has sometimes
been represented, it was not one that stood in the
main stream of things. Had Jesus appeared in Greece
or Italy, in Egypt or in India, one might have esti-
mated more highly His prospects of success. They would
have had a stage more fitted for genius than the
obscure and out-of-the-way corner of the world wherein
He played His part. Then His race was even more
against Him. The attitude of the Gentile to the Jew
was one of disgust, irritation, and contempt. The
way in which the Jews held themselves aloof from
the heathen, the anxious care they took to avoid con-
tamination from them, created a deep prejudice
against them. Their religious and ceremonial scruples,
their refusal to touch the flesh of the swine, and their
rigid observance of the Sabbath made them a butt of
constant ridicule. And the Jew met the contempt of
the heathen with a still fiercer scorn. He proudly remembered the ancient glories of his race, he looked
with contempt on the pagan religions in the consciousness that Israel alone possessed the knowledge of the
true God, and he bitterly resented the oppression of
his country by the hated Roman power. What race

would one have less expected to give a religious leader who should win to His faith the conquerors of His people ? Again, there was the disadvantage of social position. Buddha was nobly born, but Jesus belonged to the family of a village carpenter. Among His own people this would tell less against Him, for the Jews were honourably distinguished by the respect they paid to manual labour, but in the world outside there was a different scale of values, and the religion of the Carpenter seemed a fit subject for ridicule. How could God's Son have appeared in such lowly guise ? If such a thing as an Incarnation was possible at all, at least it must be attended by fit conditions of wealth and splendour. For they naturally looked for the Divine in that which was powerful and rich and magnificent, not in conditions of weakness, poverty, and humility. That the Son of God should be an artisan contradicted their prejudices as to the fitness of things.

But if His countrymen were not repelled by the fact that He was a mechanic, there was in their minds a prejudice which was likely to prove even more fatal. Jesus had received no theological education. For a religious leader this was in Judaism a very grave defect. The very type of its religion, resting as it did upon the Old Testament and especially upon the Law, gave the expert a position of great prestige and authority. The most important class of society was not the priesthood, but the scribes. In the Law of the Rabbis, Jesus had never been trained. It is a curious fact that Paul, who was trained as a Rabbi, worked mainly among Gentiles, who cared nothing about Rabbinism; whereas Jesus and the original apostles, who were untrained in Jewish theology, laboured among those who set an inordinate value upon it. Yet the word which Jesus uttered, while lacking all the authority of long-established and learned tradition, impressed the Jews with its freshness, its beauty, its originality, and, above all, with that note of independent authority which carried it straight home to the hearts of His hearers. It was, it is true, an advantage to the Gospel, when it passed into the Gentile world, that the teaching of Jesus was so free from pedantry and that it spoke the language of humanity and not the wearisome jargon of the schools. They would have turned away with impatience from a religion of hair-splitting casuistry about the trivial questions which engaged the attention of the scribes. But it was weighted with other disadvantages in its appeal to the Gentile world. Jesus was as little an expert in Greek philosophy as He was in Rabbinical learning. The Gospel did not concern itself with the questions that agitated the philosophical schools, it did not speak their technical dialect. When we think of the great names in the splendid galaxy of Greek philosophers, of Socrates and Plato and Aristotle, when we remember their long and arduous training, the width of their knowledge,

R

the keenness of their insight, their familiarity with the best that had been thought and said by their predecessors, the splendid genius which was the personal equipment of each, we realise how vast were their advantages over the uncultured Carpenter of Nazareth. And yet by common consent His artless and homely teaching strikes more truly to the core of things than the deepest teaching of the greatest masters in philosophy.

And if the Gospel was thus hampered in its appeal to the philosopher, it was similarly hampered in its appeal to the average man. For to him the new religion came stripped of the accessories with which he was most familiar. The monotheism that commended it to the Jew or the philosopher made it seem cod and forbidding to ordinary people. Its exacting standard of morality gave it an irksome and forbidding appearance. What had they to do with a religion which had no animal sacrifice, no priesthood, no temples, and thus seemed devoid of the warmth and familiarity possessed by the materialised religions to which the populace was accustomed? They could hardly realise that Christianity was a religion at all.

Once more we may remind ourselves of the extraordinary brevity of Christ's public career. It was probably embraced within a period of less than three years, whereas the work of men like Buddha and Socrates, Plato and Aristotle, was spread over a long period of intense and fruitful activity. And yet the brief span of public activity which was all that was permitted to Jesus effected a mightier revolution than the lengthiest careers of the greatest among the sons of men.

And, as if to crown all the foolishness of the story, there was the supreme folly and scandal of the Cross. What could be a fitter subject for ridicule than the story of a crucified Jewish provincial, an outcast even from His own despised people, who was proclaimed by His followers to be the Son of God ? And yet it is mere matter of history that this crazy story has been the most powerful engine of human progress and redemption which the world has known. Here, indeed, the foolishness of God has been wiser than man.

But now, with all these numerous disabilities, it would not have been wonderful if Jesus had set Himself to overcome them by enlisting on His side the sympathies of His people. It is, however, remarkable that He did not seek even this advantage. Probably He could have placed Himself at the head of a great Messian c movement, inasmuch as the patriotism of the Jews was always in a very inflammable condition. But He deliberately set Himself against the cherished prejudices of His countrymen and died a victim to their disappointment in Him. He did not court the favour o the religious leaders of His time or seek to win them to His side, He made them rather the objects of His most scathing invective. He shocked the prejudices of the religious classes by consorting with publicans and sinners.

When, then, we inquire in virtue of what it was that with everything, as it seemed, against Him He nevertheless achieved so vast a success, we can hardly find any answer other than this—that the secret of it lay in Himself. And when we ask for a formula in which our explanation may be embodied, we may find it in the Church's confession that Jesus of Nazareth is the Son of God.

And, lastly, I would call attention to the way in which the various lines of evidence that we have been pursuing converge on this conclusion. For it is not a chain of evidence which we have been following where the weakness of a single link may invalidate the whole reasoning, but we have been accumulating a large number of independent arguments, each one of which points in this direction and is supported by all the rest. We have seen reason for our belief that Jesus was gifted with miraculous power. We have further found good ground for accepting His supernatural birth and His resurrection. We have observed how the character and teaching of Jesus are each marked by internal consistency and are in mutual harmony with one another. We have seen that Jesus not only proclaimed the loftiest moral ideal, but Himself attained it. We have discovered, further, that He made on His followers the impression that He was Divine, and that He Himself, both directly and indirectly, made the same claim, and we have found a vindication of it in the place filled by Jesus in universal history in spite of the overwhelming disadvantages under which He did His work.

CHAPTER XIV

THE PROBLEM OF THE INCARNATION

OUR previous discussion has led us to accept the doctrine of the Divinity of Christ. I may linger for a moment on the importance of this before I pass on to consider the problems which it presents to us. Antecedently it would seem to us so incredible that we might well be excused for approaching the question with a large measure of incredulity, and it is all the more difficult for us, in the vast extension of our knowledge of the universe, to bring ourselves to believe it. For we no longer live in an age when the earth is regarded as the centre of the universe, with the sun and moon as its lamps, with the solid firmament overhead studded with twinkling points of light which are led out and marshalled in the sky. The progress of science has brought with it an overpowering sense of the physical insignificance of the world in which we live, and has vastly enhanced our conception of the mightiness of that Power which called it into being and leads it on its ordered way. That on our speck of stellar dust the Son of God should have become incarnate, and should have lived and died, taxes our faith too much to be readily accepted. Yet prejudice must yield to evidence, and the cogency of the evidence we have already seen. Moreover, it would be a mistake to regard physical magnitude as a criterion of spiritual worth. The single individual is worth more than the largest aggregates of unconscious matter. The greatest fact, then, in the history of our world is that the Son of God became one of ourselves, and lived and died as God manifest in the flesh. Thus He translated into our human speech the language of the Eternal. He revealed in our human conditions the inmost character of God. And He did more than this, for He assured us, by the surrender of Himself to humiliation and death, that God did not regard His world with callous indifference, but with deep compassion and love. The message of the Incarnation is that God loves us better than He loves Himself.

But, while we may affirm the fact of the Incarnation, we are confronted by perhaps insoluble difficulties as we try to apprehend the conditions that it had to satisfy and the mode in which it was achieved. We are, it may be, in a better position than at one time to understand the conditions of the problem, and this has deepened our sense of its difficulty. The essential conditions of a true solution are a full recognition of the Divinity of Christ coupled with as full a recognition of His humanity, and, on the other hand, an insistence on the unity of this Divine-human Person, with a frank acceptance of all that may be involved in the adjustment of the two factors. Now,

4   it lies in the nature of the case that such a union must be full of mystery to us, for we know only imperfectly what human nature is. We have, it is true, an immediate experience of it, but it is of a character to make the comprehension of it very difficult. The very attempt to study it invests it with artificiality. The natural is free from self-consciousness, and we can no more bend our minds to introspection without destroying the natural character of the consciousness we seek to study than we can look natural in obedience to the photographer. Moreover, recent investigation has made clear how elementary our knowledge of personality is. Here I return to considerations previously mentioned in connexion with the problem of the Divine

5   Personality. The whole series of investigations which have revealed to us the existence of the subconscious self has shown us how vast may be the realm of our personality that lies for our consciousness in deep shadow, its very existence but dimly guessed. All the acts we have ever done, the words we have spoken, the emotions we have experienced, the thoughts which have flitted in and out again, are registered there, though most of them have long since passed out of our conscious life. Yet, buried deep as they are below the surface with years of neglect and forgetfulness, the merest chance may call them back from the dead and present them vividly to our recognition. But this by no means exhausts the great treasury which we possess in that personality of ours which lies be-

neath the threshold. Much is stored there which has never been the object of our full attention at all. In every moment of our wakeful life there is an unending stream of impressions pouring in through every gateway of the senses and leaving their mark on the sensitive receivers. To most of these we pay no attention ; we can hardly be said to be aware of them. I say all this simply to indicate how little we know of human personality.

But if we know little of what personality involves in ourselves, though we really possess it, how much less do we know of personality in God ! If, then, we understand so little of the two factors themselves, how little we can penetrate the mystery of a personality in which the two factors are combined ! The entrance of the Son of God into the conditions of human life is hedged about with mystery, and the record of His earthly life presents almost insoluble difficulties. Yet we may see, to some extent, what conditions the problem involves and suggest lines along which we may move towards a solution. It would be a strange presumption that should impel us to force our way into the Holy of Holies of that Temple which was sanctified by the indwelling of the Son of God. We may put our shoes off our feet as we approach the outer courts of the sanctuary. Yet we must not tremble timidly for the Ark of God or lay profane hands on it, lest harm may befall it.

In the first place, we must assert with the utmost

firmness the reality of Christ's humanity and His participation in a real human experience. Dogmatic theologians have frequently been unfaithful to this portion of their trust. They have, it is true, formally denounced as heresy any suppression of the human factor, but they have constantly made assertions about Jesus which were not really compatible with a hearty recognition of His human limitations. Against such denials we must set the positive affirmations of the New Testament, the language of which is singularly clear and strong on this subject. Especially the Epistle to the Hebrews is valuable here in its emphatic declaration that the Son of God was made like His brethren in all points except sin. The point on which the controversy has in modern times converged has been the question of Christ's knowledge during His humiliation. In Great Britain the question has gained a practical interest on account of the progress of Biblical criticism. For my own part, I do not believe that in anything which Jesus said on the Old Testament He meant to be understood as pronouncing on the authorship of any portion of it. He used the language of His day, just as a speaker who might believe that the Homeric poems were not the work of one man might, nevertheless, speak of Homer, when referring to them, to illustrate what he might be saying. I consider it, personally, very dangerous for good people to invoke the authority of Christ to discredit critical results, and I am glad to see that Dr. Orr, who is at once an eminent theologian and one of the ablest opponents of the dominant school of Old Testament criticism, considers that the references of Christ are not to be quoted as authoritatively settling these questions.

It was not, however, Biblical criticism which forced this problem in its modern form to the front. Luther's doctrine of the Lord's Supper gave rise to his belief in the ubiquity of Christ's body through the communication to the human nature of the properties which belonged to the Divine. This doctrine has always imposed a great problem on the Lutheran Church and intensified its interest in Christology. To it we owe the various types of what are known as Kenotic theories. Even though none of them could be regarded as successful, yet they have done great service, not the least being that they have forced on our notice the existence of the problem and taught us to realise its great complexity. The term " Kenosis " is borrowed from the Greek word " to empty," which is used by Paul in his great passage in the Epistle to the Philippians, where he says of Christ that He emptied Himself. It is, of course, extremely questionable whether anything in the nature of the modern Kenotic theories was before Paul's mind when he used the term, but this need not prevent our employment of it as a convenient label. There have been several forms of this theory which would involve too much technical treatment to describe here. Those who

desire a good statement with careful criticism will
find it in Bruce's great work, *The Humiliation of
Christ*.

Our surest source of information on this subject is
the Gospel narrative. This sets before us the life of
Jesus as it was actually lived, and to this presentation
all theological preconceptions must give way. It has
been the bane of theological speculation in the past,
that it has started too often from a speculative idea
as to what is involved in the union of man with God.
It is the note of our modern study that it rests on
facts and does not permit itself to be swayed by prejudice or prepossession. Now the Gospel narrative
exhibits Jesus as human through and through. He
is bone of our bone and flesh of our flesh, and that not
only in the physical conditions, but the mental and
the spiritual. He confesses His ignorance in a matter
of high theological importance. He asks for information in such a way as to imply that He did not possess
it. We must avoid the profanity of suggesting that
He deliberately gave a false impression, nor may we
seek to save His omniscience at the expense of His
absolute truthfulness. It would be a deep disloyalty
to accuse Him of unreality. We are, in fact, shut up
to one of two conclusions—either Christ did not know
certain things, or He pretended not to know. Now,
there has been a time in the history of the Church
when men have been so keenly alive to theological
that they were dull to moral considerations, and actu-

ally uttered such statements as that Christ usefully pretended not to know. Happily such a saying would now be felt to be an outrage on the veracity of our Lord, even by those who do not realise that the only alternative to it is to accept quite frankly the limitations of His knowledge. The supernatural knowledge which Jesus displays forms part of the miraculous element which marked His career, and was not a personal equipment for His own use, but, so to speak, an official endowment for the ends of His mission. It belongs to the same type as the supernatural knowledge which we find possessed by the prophets, though naturally surpassing it.

We may see with especial clearness what is involved in this respect if we consider the significance of the fact that He was tempted in all points like as we are. This in itself involves a limitation in His knowledge. This can be best seen from a temptation which is among the most urgent we have to meet. It is one which presses with most severity upon those who are most deeply filled with the love of their fellows. It is also one of the most critical and dangerous, since it strikes at the very vitals of religion. It must, therefore, have been experienced by Christ, otherwise He would have been untested in one of the conflicts where the trial is most severe. And in virtue of the boundless love that possessed Him, the depth of His pity, the richness of His sympathy, the keenness of His imagination, it must have pressed upon Him with a peculiar intensity. The temptation to which I refer springs out of the undeserved suffering, the brutal oppression and injustice, which confront us on every hand. The question that springs to our lips as the spectacle forces itself upon us in all its accumulated horror is whether a world such as this can be governed by a holy and a loving God. Such a temptation appeals but little to those of coarse and dull sensibilities, to the apathetic and unimaginative. It does not rack the self-centred, who trouble but little for the welfare of others provided their own comfort is undisturbed. But to a spirit so constituted as that of Jesus we can only faintly conceive with what appalling force such a temptation would come. And now, how does the Christian hold fast his faith in God when he is assailed by this temptation ? He may, of course, on this line or that, mitigate the pressure of the difficulty by pointing to various considerations which tend to relieve it. But when all has been said of which the case admits, he has still to leave a realm of mystery. In the face of so much that shows us unspeakable wretchedness in the world he meets its suggestion of unbelief with the answer that it is only our ignorance which prevents us from seeing God's love even in spite of this. If we knew as God knows, we too should know that the world's evil does not contradict the love of God. But this means that the temptation would have no significance for us were it not for our ignorance. Inasmuch, then, as Christ must have been tempted in this vital point as we are, He must have shared the ignorance which alone made such a temptation possible.

But not only does the New Testament clearly reveal to us a Jesus who grew in wisdom and knowledge, and one who was limited as we are on the intellectual side, it also depicts Him as standing with us in His relationship to God. He used the ordinary means of grace, nurtured His spiritual life on Scripture and fellowship with God, and met the assaults of the tempter with the sword of the Spirit. The author of the Epistle to the Hebrews insists that, like His brethren, He praised God in the congregation and reposed in Him His human trust. But now the question may be asked : Does not this detract from the real greatness of Christ ? It is surely obvious, on the contrary, that it enhances it. We do not consider, when one makes a great surrender of social position and wealth, or of the possibilities of knowledge which open up before him, in order that he may give his life to the debased, that he is the less to be honoured for doing so. When one who might have been a great scholar, and whose instincts draw him powerfully towards such a career, turns resolutely away from these tempting paths that he may become a missionary to the heathen or the outcast, the ignorance of much which he might otherwise have known is no reproach but a title to our regard. And so the Son of God seems the more glorious for His ignorance, since it proves that He set the salvation of men before the jealous guarding of His own prerogatives.

14 Yet the question might still arise whether this limitation does not impair His Divinity. We might, of course, ask whether each of the Persons in the Trinity possessed, in virtue of His intrinsic being, each of the attributes which belong to God considered as a unity. We ought, perhaps, not rashly to assume that omniscience is a quality possessed by each of the Persons of the Godhead in His own right. Of course, in virtue of the mutual indwelling and perfect communion of life which exists in the circle of the Godhead the omniscience of the Father would be shared by the Son and Spirit. But if it was not a quality which belonged to His essential being, but one which He enjoyed through His communion with the Father's life, it would help us to understand how He might renounce the enjoyment of it without impairing the intrinsic quality of His being. It may be urged that this is of so speculative a character that no importance can be attached to it. Very good, but it is important in this respect, that it at least shows the possibility of an interpretation other than that which is commonly assumed as self-evident. I am not for one moment suggesting that this has really happened; obviously in a matter of this kind we have no information to guide us.

15 The real answer, however, to the objection is, I think, to be sought in a more correct definition of what

we mean by Divinity, what it is which makes God to be God. We confess that God is the All-powerful and All-wise, but it is not in these qualities that the essence of His Divinity resides, but in those which are moral and spiritual. He is perfect in holiness and in love. We could think of an evil being endowed with omnipotence and omniscience giving all the more terrible expression to his essential devilishness that he was unrestricted by limitations in power or in knowledge. If we are seeking the definition of God, we must place at the very centre of it those qualities which could not be possessed by that which was in essence undivine and which could not be surrendered without loss of the necessary quality of deity. The New Testament has taught us to recognise that God is Love. Browning has expressed the truth in his lines :—

> A loving worm within its clod,
> Were diviner than a loveless God
> Amid His worlds I would dare to say.

I urge, then, that the less essential qualities may be surrendered without impairing what is essentially Divine if they are surrendered in order that the divinest qualities may receive enhancement. If they are sacrificed that love may gain a larger scope and a deeper satisfaction, we must recognise in that no loss of Divinity, but rather the winning by Godhood of yet fuller and more congenial expression. And thus Jesus, as He lived on earth, a weak, mortal man, sharing our ignorance, and compassed with our in-

s

firmity, was not the less God, but the more God, because the love that made Him God had risen to the most God-like surrender.

> I never realised God's birth before,
> How He grew likest God in being born.

CHAPTER XV

THE WORK OF CHRIST

FROM the thought of the Incarnation our minds turn reverently to the Passion and Resurrection of our Lord. It may seem to some as if here the voice of Theology should be hushed, and the Spirit of Devotion take up the strain. We draw near the Holy of Holies with our shoes off our feet and with the Song of the Redeemed on our lips. Here it is fitting that controversy should die into silence, that we should stand with the Beloved Disciple beneath the Cross, or take our place with the apostles as the Risen One is revealed to our gaze. But while we must never forget the true temper of devotion in all our probing of the intellectual mystery, it would be a mistaken reverence to imagine that we did most homage to the Cross by renouncing the attempt to understand it. For it is as its secret becomes disclosed to us that we feel the spell of its power. And it is the more necessary to insist on this since some who feel acutely the difficulties of the theme adopt an attitude of despair and urge that we should be content with asserting the fact of the Atonement without seeking to construct a theory.

We are intellectually so constituted that we cannot permanently be content to place in the centre of our message something of which we can give no rational account. Of course, it is not our view of the Atonement that saves us, and it would be an evil day for the future of Christianity when the acceptance of a particular theory of the work of Christ should be made necessary to salvation. We have had too much of that folly in the past, but the mistakes of our predecessors ought to be a warning to ourselves. The fundamental thing to believe is that it is God in Christ who saves us. This is all that is necessary for saving faith. The soul casts itself in trust upon Christ, and need have formulated no scheme of doctrine in order to account for the possibility of its experience. The message of Christ is not " Believe in this doctrine or that," but " Believe in Me." But while for the individual sinner who is seeking salvation a theory of the Atonement is unnecessary, the theologian cannot afford to do without it. And even the ordinary Christian, on whom the burden of constructing a system of doctrine does not rest, will find that his hold on Christian truth is deepened and his religious life is strengthened if he does not relegate the fact of salvation to the realm of the unintelligible, but seeks to reach a clear perception of its meaning. Naturally we must leave room for a large element of mystery. They have not been the best friends of Christian truth who have constructed a theory of the Atonement as lucid and as inevitable as the multiplication table. We are dealing here with the deep secrets of the Divine counsel, and must reverently guard ourselves against the lack of modesty displayed by those who profess to explain everything. Yet we must not be daunted by these considerations, and renounce the attempt to gain any insight into the principles that came to expression in the work of Christ. In the presence of these august realities in which God is doing His mightiest work what can we be but humbled and abashed, conscious how little we are able to fathom His impenetrable designs? To the mind of antiquity it seemed to be dangerous to catch the Divinity at work. And though we have been emancipated from these superstitious terrors and live in the glad freedom of the children of God, no longer avoiding His presence, but welcomed to His breast, we may yet learn the lesson that it does not become us to peer with profane curiosity into the inmost secrets of His action. Yet where He has Himself graciously disclosed to us somewhat of the mysteries of His working we may reverently seek to understand His ways. For while a god whom we fully understood could be no god to us, with a god whom we did not understand at all we could have no religious relations.

It is all the more important to insist on this since there is a widespread tendency to reject with indifference the doctrine of the Atonement. If we examine into the causes of this, we find that they may be roughly classed under two heads. A very large number reject the doctrine owing to the fact that they have identified it with a particular theory in which they have probably been brought up, and are ignorant of the well-known fact that there is no such thing as an orthodox theory of the Atonement. The historian knows well enough what numerous theories have been formulated, under what varying impulses, and with what strange results. He is, therefore, well aware that the identification of any theory with the fact cannot be made legitimately a test of orthodoxy. The practical mischief has been that in sheer ignorance many have abandoned the fact because they could not honestly accept the theory which they erroneously imagined to be identical with it. But there are others who reject the fact itself because it does not harmonise with the theological or philosophical presuppositions with which they approach it. But frequently these presuppositions have been unconsciously accepted as axiomatic without any suspicion that they needed to be very critically examined. We have certain ideas that exist as the outcome of experience in very rough-and-ready form which we unhesitatingly apply as touchstones of the truth of such doctrines as that of the Atonement. But we need to remember, in the first place, that our human experience gives us these ideas, not in their pure, essential meaning, but often in very crude and misleading forms. We need to see them, not as they emerge in our human conditions, but as they are in themselves. That is why it happens that human analogies have frequently proved misleading, because the principles which they have only caricatured have been transferred in their caricatured form to problems which are patient of them only in their ideal form. It is, no doubt, quite possible to do something towards disengaging the essential truth from its crude embodiment, and seeing it from the point of view of the ideal spectator. Yet it is plain that in trying to do so we should practise constant self-distrust.

And when a more adequate doctrine is at last constructed we may anticipate that several factors will go to its making. First of all, the deeper insight into Scripture which the last century brought with it will provide us with richer material and material better understood. We shall not, as the older theologians did, construct a patchwork by taking elements indiscriminately from all parts of the Bible, and then, piecing them together into a whole, call this ill-assorted mixture the Biblical doctrine of the Atonement. On the contrary, we shall follow the method of Biblical Theology and study each section in and for itself. We shall come to the New Testament through a careful investigation into the history of the religion of Israel in which we shall mark the contribution made by the great individual writers, and study with what thoroughness we can the history of the religious institutions and, in this connexion especially, the sacri-

ficial system. Then, when we come to the New
Testament, we shall be similarly discriminating. We
shall seek to understand the different types of teaching it contains—the teaching of Jesus, of Paul, of John,
of Peter, and of the Epistle to the Hebrews. When
that has been accomplished, the next step will be to
work these different systems into a connected scheme
that our theory may be marked by the largeness and
many-sided character which belongs to the New
Testament as a whole. For, happily, the New Testament presents us with a treatment of the problem
from several different points of view, so that what
could not be adequately seen from one standpoint
should have justice done to it from another. Then
we shall follow the course of the doctrine as it has been
developed in Christian thought, and thus learn how
the needs of the Church and various types of experience have created for themselves congenial forms of
statement. Nor shall we be indifferent to the light
that has been cast by philosophy and especially by
the study of ethics upon the problem. All the difficult
questions which cluster about forgiveness, for example,
must be taken into account by the systematic theologian as he seeks to accomplish his task. Moreover,
he must not sink below the moral standard of his own
time ; he must be sensitive to the demand that the
action of God shall be exhibited in harmony with the
most elevated morality. He must not permit himself
to think that immorality ceases to be immorality

could never have originated except from an attempt to work out to its logical issues what seemed to be implied in the Biblical metaphor of ransom. I do not, of course, intend that we should empty Biblical language of its meaning. But we should ascertain that meaning in the light of the fact that the Bible is the people's and not simply the theologian's book.

Naturally the present discussion does not carry out the ambitious programme I have sketched, but a wholesome reminder of the lines on which an adequate theory must be constructed is not irrelevant, since it warns us against undue haste and superficiality. With these thoughts in our mind we may approach the consideration of our theme.

Theology has often suffered from undue limitations in its conception of the work of Christ by concentrating attention too exclusively upon His death. It is well, therefore, at the outset to insist on the largeness of the work accomplished by Him. Many have spoken as though the purpose of the Incarnation was exhausted in the Atonement, as if Jesus was born merely that He might die. But we have to find the work of Jesus not simply in redemption, but also in revelation. He came, first of all, to reveal the nature of God. He lived the Divine life under our human limitations, and thus translated the ineffable qualities of the Divine into a human life and character which even the least intelligent could love and reverence and in his measure understand. But He revealed also the true ideal of humanity. He showed us not only what God is, but what we ought to be. He set the perfect standard in religion and conduct alike, so that in our moral and spiritual efforts we might have a goal before us to guide us aright. Moreover, even the work of redemption is too often confined to the death of Christ. This, however, is unscriptural. The New Testament lays very great stress in this connexion upon Christ's resurrection, not simply as something that attests the claims which Jesus made for Himself, or cancels the curse upon Him involved in His death, but as an integral part of the work of salvation. Further, we cannot detach the death of Christ from His life. The Incarnation was itself a sacrifice, and the sacrificial quality penetrated the whole of His earthly career. No doubt there is a peculiar significance attached to the experience of Calvary, but we impoverish the Gospel when we fix our gaze on Calvary with such intensity as to be blind to the significance of Bethlehem and Galilee, the empty grave and the Mount of Olives. Many theologians have, in fact, held that, even had there been no sin, the Incarnation would still have been necessary in order to complete our humanity and perfectly reveal God. This raises, of course, a purely theoretical issue, since, if what I have said of the Pauline doctrine of sin is correct, sin was an inevitable stage in the moral development of mankind. But I mention it as illustrating the truth that the Incarnation was intended to serve other purposes than the redemption of the world from sin. But we have, in fact, to deal with a sinful world which is the subject of redemption, and it is here that the difficulties of our subject are really felt.

Nowhere do we see more clearly the truth that the working out of the theological system depends on the conception of God than in the doctrine of the Atonement. We must beware of representing God in an unholy light, as a sullen or a punctilious, a self-seeking or a vindictive Being. We must not so emphasise His unbending justice as to forget His mercy and His love, nor, on the other hand, imagine Him to be a merely good-natured, indulgent Deity. We do best when we cleave most closely to Christ's thoughts of God. Now the thought on which Christ most loved to dwell was the Fatherhood of God. It is often urged that this is an inadequate conception, since the relations of God to the race are wider than the relations of a father to a family. But it is very significant that Jesus threw into prominence the idea of Fatherhood and laid little, if any, stress on conceptions which have been allowed to dominate theology. I do not myself think it is quite reverent for Christ's followers to belittle His fundamental conceptions in this way, and the answer to the difficulty that is urged must be sought in a more comprehensive definition of Fatherhood. What was central and fundamental to Him, who knew God as no one else has known Him, must be central and fundamental to us.

From this point of view, then, we must, in harmony with the New Testament, regard the Atonement as pre-eminently the outcome of God's grace and love. This at once frees us from the pagan notion which has played so large a part in popular ideas that the death of Christ was necessary to appease an angry God. The truth is, rather, that the death of Christ could never have taken place had not God's attitude to mankind been one of yearning love. Yet we must not cheapen the idea of love. The love of God is holy love. His righteousness must set Him in unrelenting conflict with sin. Nay, we must not shrink from speaking of the anger of God. A being incapable of moral indignation, who could look upon oppression and wrong without feeling anger at those who perpetrated it, would be too morally base to deserve the title of God. But even the anger and the holiness and the righteousness, if we can only understand it, are elements in the consuming fire of His love. The Father sees mankind as His children, the victims of sin. His chief concern is for their good, how the sin which has blighted their character may become a thing of the past. And it is in the death and resurrection of Christ that the Gospel finds God's answer to this problem.

Now the first stage in the upward path is to bring the sinner to realise the true nature of his sin. Paul attaches great importance to the recognition of sin's real character. He points out that it was one of the functions of the Law to reveal the exceeding sinfulness of sin. Sin pressed the holy Law of God into its unhallowed service, and thus, by perverting that Law into its tool, it revealed its own intrinsic baseness. Christ's first work is to convict the world of sin, and He does this in various ways. First of all, by the shock of contrast between our character and His own. As we consider the perfect beauty of His life we are awakened to the imperfection of our own. And, secondly, by His exhibition of the nature and love of God. For here again the contrast between the holiness of our heavenly Father and our own evil nature brings home to us a sense of the moral difference which lies between us, while the revelation of God's love displays the unfilial ingratitude of our rebellion. But this revelation finds its climax in the death of Christ. The fact that sinful man could so handle the Holy One of God revealed as nothing else could do sin's dark malignity. And, on the other hand, the fact that to save man from sin God surrendered His Son to death showed how virulent He deemed the poison to be with which mankind was infected. It is very important to lay stress on this aspect of our theme. In our everyday life we know how vital it is to awaken the offender to the real gravity of his offence. And the task is peculiarly difficult. It is one of the worst features of sin that it drugs the sinner's conscience. It numbs his perception of the mischief which is at work within him. Hence he is light-hearted about it, is not dissatisfied with himself, and the more habituated he becomes to evil the less the concern it gives him. But if he has any capacity for amendment, the conscience is likely to be stirred by the spectacle of the ruin and havoc which is wrought by his sin. Not, indeed, that this is invariably the case. For many seem to pass beyond the stage at which even this causes them disquiet. But this may help us to understand one of the functions fulfilled by the Cross. Once we have realised that it was sin which crucified the sinless One we understand as never before its intrinsic character.

And thus repentance is created. It is often said, Why should not God forgive the sinner when he repents without any necessity for the death of Christ? Those who argue in this way have probably not asked themselves how much is implied in the condition which they lay down. Is repentance so easy, so commonplace a matter? A superficial repentance is not difficult. But when we talk of repentance we ought to mean something much more than that. We ought to mean a clear perception of the gravity of our fault. We must recognise our desperate case, understand how deeply the cancer has eaten into our soul, think of all the wilfulness and blindness, the ingratitude and selfishness which our life of sin day after day and year after year has involved. It is not a situation to be dealt with by apologies or regrets. It is something that demands a passionate sorrow, a whole-hearted abhorrence of our evil past, a hearty acceptance of God's standpoint with reference to our sin. Indeed, it is often only as the Christian life itself expands and deepens that repentance begins to become at all adequate. It is the saint who is the true penitent, and seeing that the task of repentance is so difficult, when we have rightly understood what it involves, we shall distrust all rose-water methods of tinkering with the disease.

But the question arises at this point, Is repentance in this deep, full sense an adequate ground of forgiveness? Is the Cross of Christ simply an instrument for creating penitence, or is it something more? I think we are not faithful to the New Testament standpoint unless we recognise that it is something more. Forgiveness is not something to be taken for granted too easily. The parable of the Prodigal Son expresses in the most beautiful way the love and welcome which is in the Father's heart. But that love, just because it is love, must be holy, righteous love, and it is a perilous thing to build the whole doctrine of salvation on a single parable, as if this exhausted the whole message of the Gospel. Paul brings out one very important element in his famous passage on the new righteousness in the third chapter of Romans. There was a danger lest God's forbearance in the past should lead men to misinterpret His clemency as indifference to sin. Such a misconception struck a blow at the vitals of ethical religion, and therefore Paul explains God's action in the death of Christ as designed to vindicate

T

Him from the charge of such moral indifference. Even at this tremendous cost it had to be made plain that God did not palter with moral considerations. The Cross of Christ is the vindication of God's Holiness. And we ourselves recognise it to be true that an easy forgiveness may be a sign of moral shallowness. It may mean that the injured person has no adequate appreciation of the gravity of the offence. He forgives so easily because for him the wrong is so trivial. An adequate forgiveness must include a full recognition of the heinousness of the act. In our own case it is so easy to mask unworthy resentment behind the plea of a love for justice that we must always be on our guard against a grudging forgiveness. But the ideal attitude is that the heart should always be ready to forgive even while the forgiveness itself must wait for a sufficient penitence. It is not good for the transgressor that he should be forgiven on too easy terms, or his moral standard tends to be degraded. And God, in whom there is no trace of resentment, but whose whole heart moves with love towards the sinful, must yet, because He is the holy God and because His love seeks the sinner's highest good, wait to forgive till the claims of His own imperious righteousness are satisfied. And so we may say that, while God's action is always prompted by His love, it is always conditioned by His righteousness.

It has been held by many that the right word in which to express the essence of the Atonement is substitution. The sinner has broken the holy law of God, and our moral instincts recognise the justice of penalty for the offence. And since man could not cancel his guilt there was no way of deliverance from punishment open to him, unless that punishment was vicariously borne by one to whom it was not due. Hence the Son of God became man in order that He might bear the penalty which should be inflicted upon us. So justice was satisfied and salvation was procured. I do not deny that this theory has within it a strong element of appeal, and that, preached with fervour and conviction, it has often won the sinner from his evil way. But it has done this in virtue of the elements of truth which it contains in common with other presentations, not in virtue of the weaknesses which a more careful scrutiny cannot fail to discover in it. I can even recognise for it a relative justification, but we must go beneath it if we are to reach the truth. It is often thought that we are committed to some theory of this kind by the language of Paul. I am convinced, however, that this is not the case. Had the question been put to Paul—Did Christ die in our stead ?—I think he would have answered that in a certain sense this statement might pass, but the very putting of it implied that the real significance of the death of Christ had not been correctly apprehended. It is not Paul's deepest word on this subject.

The objections to the substitution theory are clear. In the first place, such a theory is not found in Scripture. We learn that Christ died on our behalf; we do not read that He died in our stead. If it is replied that Christ's death is represented as a sacrifice, I must simply point out that Hebrew sacrifice was in no sense substitutionary in character. In the second place, punishment cannot properly be transferred. If it is inflicted on the innocent while the guilty go free, it ceases to be punishment, and justice receives a double wound. In the next place, the theory is not in harmony with the facts. The penalties of sin were not endured by Christ, nor do we escape from them in virtue of His death. The worst penalty of sin Christ could not in the nature of the case endure. For sin brings with it its own punishment in the alienation and hatred of God which it produces, in the blunting of moral feeling, in the sense of personal guilt, in the wretchedness of a soul out of harmony with itself. These things Christ could not endure, nor could He endure such penalties in the after-life as are usually associated with sin. Neither in quantity nor in duration were the sufferings He endured co-extensive with the effects which sin brings upon the human race. And, on the other hand, it remains true just as before that we feel in ourselves the baleful effects of our transgressions, our vices do not cease to scourge us, the body and the mind bear on them the wounds of moral defeat, and we all have at last to pay the common debt of Nature. Nor do our difficulties cease here. For if Christ endured the whole penalty of sin, then it can no longer be inflicted on the sinful. And this logically involves one of two alternatives. Either we must say with the Calvinists that the Atonement is limited, that Christ died for the elect; or if, in deference to the plain statements of Scripture, we assert the universality of the Atonement, then we must infer the salvation of all, independently of character. For if Christ has exhausted all the penalty in His own Person, then none remains to be inflicted on those for whom He died, and it violates the elementary instincts of justice that the full punishment should be twice exacted for the same sin. If, in reply to this, it be said that unbelief justifies the repetition of the punishment, I must point out that this cannot be conceded. For if Christ bore the whole penalty of sin, He bore the penalty of the sinner's unbelief. Paul has drawn for us, clearly and sharply, the distinction between debt and grace and shown us that they are mutually incompatible, and we must refrain from introducing the old contradiction in a new form.

How, then, shall we formulate a theory that escapes the objections to which the substitutionary theory is exposed, while at the same time we maintain the truth that it seeks to express? Let us go back to the discussion of Paul's doctrine touching Adam and Christ. We saw that he regarded the act of Adam not as an individual, but as a racial act. He did not say Adam sinned in our stead and we bear the penalty. He said rather Adam's sin was our sin.

We must accordingly explain the work of Christ upon similar lines. His death was our death. It was no individual act, but was the act of the whole human race. This is what Paul meant when he said, "We thus judge that if one died for all, then all died." He meant that on the Cross it was not Jesus of Nazareth alone, but Christ, who embraced within Himself all humanity, that suffered and died. In this experience Jesus made Himself one with us and He made us one with Himself. He made Himself one with us. In a deep and true sense He had been one with us from the beginning. We were created in Him, and He was the Head of every man. Even before He became incarnate He was our brother, and became incarnate because He honoured the fraternal tie. And in His human life He identified Himself to the utmost extent with His brethren. He shared all our infirmities and felt the strain of all our temptations. He knew pain and suffering, scorn and rejection, desertion and betrayal.

And it is especially in its relation to sin that the problem concerns us. He was the sinless One, and therefore He could not know by experience the stain of evil in His own spirit, nor could He repent for His own guilt. Yet He must acquaint Himself with our burden that He might truly bear it. And this was one of the most terrible elements in His trial. Just as we recoil from what creates physical disgust, so Jesus recoiled from sin. But He braced Himself to

face it that He might know its uttermost evil. And
as He faced it His horror deepened. He felt keen
agony for the wrong inflicted on God and for all the
incalculable evil it wrought among men. He saw it
all with a lucidity of sinless vision undimmed by any
shortcoming in Himself. But He felt not pain only,
but shame. For the shadow of all these nameless un-
numbered evils was cast upon Himself. It was His
own brothers who had age after age built that dark
and bewildering labyrinth of evil through whose mazes
He forced His shuddering soul to pass. For He must
know our sin, know it not as an abstraction or a vague
generalisation, but as a concrete hideous reality.
What wonder that, sickened by the horror of it, He
fell into an agony and prayed that the cup might pass
from Him!

But more than this was necessary. He must not
only familiarise Himself with the repulsive character
of sin; He must know also what sin involved. He
must come as close as possible to us in His experience
of the consequences of sin. Some of the older theologians, in their coarse way, with their mind fastened
on material suffering, spoke of Jesus as enduring on
the Cross all the pains of the damned. The expression
was crude; there was upon it the taint of commer-
cialism; beneath it lay the thought that the pain
endured must be the equivalent of the pain which
would have been endured by those whom He saved.
But there was a real meaning underlying all the

mythology of the expression. It was part of His identification with us that He should know, so far as a sinless being could know, the wages of sin. He must taste the last dregs in the cup. The utmost evil is the separation which sin creates between man and God, that is the true death, and this death Jesus died before He yielded His spirit into His Father's hands. As He goes forward with the work of human redemption, bearing with fortitude not only the physical pain, but the deep mental agony for sin, wrestling with principalities and powers, and conscious of God's approval, there comes upon Him with a bewildering shock the sense that His Father, who had been with Him and on whom He had always stayed His soul, had withdrawn from Him. It was not that God had ceased to sympathise and approve ; it was that the deepest consequence of sin might not be evaded. This was the sharpest of all the pangs which Jesus was called upon to suffer, and this He endured because He made Himself one with us.

Christ, then, knowing sin as He did, recognising all its virulence and its deep disloyalty, assents with all His strength to the condemnation God passes upon it, and accepts the consequence to which it leads. But His act is the act of the race, and thus in Him the race confesses its guilt and accepts the consequences. And so God passes a new judgment upon the race, no longer the judgment of condemnation, but the judgment of approval. He sees the race, not as it stood in the First, but as it stands in the Second Man.

It may be said, Is not this a fanciful theory with no correspondence in actual fact ? What are we to make of the idea that in the death of Jesus humanity died ? I do not think that the term " representative," which sufficed to define the relation in which Paul conceived the first Adam to stand to us, is adequate to depict the relation between Christ and the race. Christ is more than our representative. Indeed, had He been no more He could not have represented us. For it is quite clear, as we look abroad at the world, that a sinless holy Being stands apart from us by so deep a gulf that He cannot be fitly said to represent us. And yet an original relation subsists between Christ and the race. It strikes its roots into the Second as it does into the First Adam. It is this relation which provides the basis for the Incarnation. But in order that He might achieve the work of our redemption He had not simply to stand for us, but to become one with us. The term we need to express this is not representation, but identification. He became so one with us as to assume all our responsibilities, and, so to speak, by a dead lift to raise us out of the horrible pit and the miry clay.

The thought of solidarity, of our union and mutual responsibility, is one on which our own age lays great stress, but which is also to be found in the New Testament. Paul insists that we are all members one of

another, and that nothing can overtake the individual
without affecting the collective body. We see how
the sin of one often involves many more in the suffering it entails. There is a deep truth in the idea of
vicarious suffering as seen in everyday life. It is our
constant experience to see the innocent suffer for the
guilty. But it is questionable how far we can speak
of this as effecting Atonement. The spectacle of it
may awaken the evildoer to the true character of his
offence, but once his conscience is aroused it will be
difficult to convince him that the suffering of others
has lightened the guilt that he has to bear. For they
stand distinct one from another, and in the moral sphere
no transference of merit is possible. Indeed, there is
no superfluous merit to be transferred. And once we
have understood the true relations between man and
God we can see that the idea that any one can be better
than he ought to be is an absurdity. And this is true
of Jesus. He was bound in His duty to God to be as
good as it was possible for Him to be, and it is a mere
fiction to suppose, as Anselm did, that Jesus went
beyond what was required of Him when, although
death had no claim on the sinless, He died in obedience
to the Father's will. Indeed, we are discussing the
subject on the wrong plane when we treat it as a
question of merit at all. But what is not possible
where there is separation becomes possible with identification. It is possible for Jesus to suffer on our behalf,
and for the benefits of that suffering to be appropriated

by us, because He is one with the race for which He dies. But we must be prepared to carry that identification through to its conclusion. If Jesus really united Himself to humanity, then He made the lot of humanity His own. And this at once widens our whole conception of His work. I have already urged that we must not interpret that work too narrowly as concentrated in His death.

But now I wish to extend this principle further, and to urge that we must regard the suffering of Christ as co-extensive with the suffering of the race. Calvary is the climax and classical example of a process co-extensive with human history. And thus He works into His own redeeming pain the sorrows and sufferings endured by the human race through all time. It is not that these sufferings have redemptive value in themselves, but they gain it because they become the sufferings of Christ. Thus it is in Christ, and in Him alone, that mankind achieves redemption, but its own suffering receives a new dignity and is endowed with a higher purpose in that it is thus taken up by Christ and made part of His own redemptive achievement. Thus God sees at work another tendency in the race which reverses His own judgment about it from condemnation to justification.

But the problem is not simply one of death for sin. There is something even deeper than the cleansing from sin's guilt, and that is the breaking of sin's power. We have to lay stress on the thought, which was very important to Paul, but has often been neglected in Christian teaching, that the death of Christ was not only a death for sin, but a death to sin. Paul tells us, " The death that He died, He died unto sin once." This, of course, cannot mean that by His death Christ, who had been subject to the dominion of sin, escaped from it, inasmuch as He knew no sin. But, once again, He identified Himself with the sinful race, and through this experience of death broke for Himself and for humanity the connexion with sin which this entailed. This was accomplished through the destruction of the flesh, that element in man wherein sin had its seat. The flesh was nailed to the Cross, and with it the Law which gave sin its power. Thus not only was the debt against us cancelled, but the slavery in which we were held by sin was brought to an end. But this is only one side of Paul's statement. We need not only the negative deliverance from sin, we need the positive life of holiness. And it is here that Paul's doctrine of Christ's resurrection comes as the counterpart to the doctrine of His death. Not only did Christ die to sin, but " the life that He liveth, He liveth unto God." One might, indeed, almost say that Paul attaches more importance to the resurrection than to the death of Jesus. " If while we were enemies we were reconciled unto God through the death of His Son, much more being reconciled shall we be saved by His life "—that is, His risen life. If Christ died for our sins He was also raised again for our justification. When the apostle puts the question, " Who is he that shall condemn ? " he answers, " It is Christ Jesus that died, yea, rather, that was raised from the dead." There is an energy inherent in the resurrection of Christ, and it is, therefore, Paul's aim to experience " the power of His resurrection." If, then, the death closes the old chapter of sin and disobedience, the resurrection opens the new chapter of holiness and a life unto God, and that for the race just as the death. And it must be clearly borne in mind that it is only of the race as a race that I have so far been speaking. How the racial experiences are appropriated by the individual is the question that will next engage our attention.

CHAPTER XVI

PERSONAL SALVATION

SO far we have looked at the work of Christ as a racial process. He identifies Himself with humanity, assumes its nature, participates in its experience, takes on Himself its responsibilities, familiarises Himself with its dark, sinful record, heartily assents to God's absolute condemnation of sin, and drinks without flinching the bitter cup of sin's consequences. And thus He dies for sin and to sin, blots out its guilt and annihilates its power, and initiates a new life of holiness to God. And since He thus made Himself one with man, the race that was in Him was freed from its guilt and from the tyranny of sin's dominion, and there opened up before it a life of harmony with God's will. But now we have to advance a step further and ask how the individual appropriates the blessings thus achieved.

It is through the application to his case of principles with which we have now become familiar that each has to win the blessing of personal salvation. Now the fundamental thought of Paul is not that of justification by faith. That is an important but none the less a subordinate element in Paul's doctrine. It is a consequence deduced from his central conception of union with Christ, and it is along the lines of this thought that we must construct our doctrine if we would be true to the New Testament and hold the faith in its right proportions. It is most necessary for us at this point not to tone down the apostle's teaching or seek to make it more acceptable to commonplace modes of thought. We must not allow ourselves to be satisfied with the thought that Paul means simply a moral union. He means something much deeper than that, and his language can be satisfied only by the assertion of a mystical union. Here we are moving in a region which, in the nature of the case, is very obscure, and it is very tempting to listen to the voices that recall us from these dimly lighted ways into the clear and frosty daylight. They warn us that we are only following a will-o'-the-wisp, and that we should renounce the quest into which we have been deluded. I do not deny that a moral union is an inspiring ideal, but I am sure that it is inadequate for the great mass of mankind. For what is it that we need ? We need something more than the experience that our sins are forgiven, we need to escape from the slavery in which our will is bound, and live the life of active obedience to God. If, then, I am told that the Christian life is one of moral union with Christ I acknowledge the loftiness of the standard; but I ask, Where may I gain the strength to attain it ? If the answer comes that the message and experience of forgiveness itself fills the soul with gratitude and ardent love to Him who has achieved my deliverance, far be it from me to speak lightly of such a motive. But I am compelled to dissent from those who consider that this is adequate.

It is just the people who need it most who will be least able to make use of it. Given a lofty morality to begin with, a natural disposition sensitive to love's appeal for whole-hearted response, and there we have the conditions in which gratitude can do much. But we need a Gospel for the degraded—for those whose will is weak, whose standard of morality is not naturally high, whose sense of gratitude is thin and ineffective, whose passions are strong and whose self-control is weak. And it is not to men of this kind that we can safely preach the Gospel of forgiveness and leave gratitude to do the rest. No message of moral union is here sufficient when the very problem to be solved is, How is the moral union in such cases to be attained? And not only is a moral union insufficient to meet the case, but it is an utterly inadequate explanation of the New Testament language. If the New Testament does not teach the mystical union of the believer with Christ, I do not quite understand what human language could be chosen which would express that idea. The Pauline language is so explicit that no one would have thought of challenging the interpretation had not the idea itself been objectionable, and the Johannine language harmonises well with it. Paul felt that it was no longer he that lived, but Christ that lived in him. He asserted in the most definite language, " He that is joined to the Lord is one spirit." Again and again he speaks of the Christian as " in Christ," and uses language which is emptied largely of its meaning unless it is a mystical union that he has in view. I freely grant that the conception is difficult. We are moving here in a region remote from our everyday life. We are wrestling with the deepest mysteries of spiritual experience, we are touching the profound problems as to the nature of personality and as to the relation in which as men we stand to Christ. This should absolve us from the reproach of obscurity, especially when we remember that a Gospel which left no place for mystery could hardly in the nature of things be true. The mysterious is not the irrational, and the deepest secrets of the Christian consciousness will not be adequately expressed in terms of shallow lucidity. We are dealing here with an experience that has no counterpart in our ordinary life, and we must therefore not shrink from language which is itself abnormal.

The Christian life, then, fundamentally is a life in which the human spirit is blended with Christ, and blended so intimately that he and Christ are one. Now just as the identification of Christ with the race carried with it that the race passed through the redemptive experiences through which Christ passed, so the union of the individual with Christ carries with it

U

a similar participation in His experience. He suffers with Christ, he dies with Christ, he is raised with Christ, he shares with Him His Ascension and sits with Him in heavenly places. Christ has to suffer in each of His members, each has his appointed portion to endure, and for each before his earthly pilgrimage is done there is still left to be filled up that which is lacking of Christ's sufferings in his flesh. The believer also dies with Christ. Just as ideally he was part of the race which was crucified in Christ on Calvary, so in actual experience he knows what it is to be crucified with Christ. And thus his sufferings and death, becoming through this mystical union the sufferings and death of Christ, work out results worthy of Him whose sufferings they thus become. They, too, are woven into Christ's redemptive plan, not simply for the individual who endures them, but also for the Church which is His body. In this crucifixion with Christ he realises that his old nature is put to death, that he has atoned for its sin, and that its power for him is broken. So, too, he shares in the resurrection of Christ, and from the old life of sin and moral paralysis he enters on the new life of holiness, of moral energy and victory, and a will wholly attuned to the will of God.

The apostle tells us that if any man has realised this mystical union with Christ " he is a new creature, the old things have passed away, behold they have become new." There is, first of all, the change in man's status before God. The old condition was one of guilt and condemnation, the new is one of forgiveness and justification. In two striking verses Paul has asserted this connexion between the union with Christ and the believer's status before God. Putting it in a negative form, he says, " There is no condemnation for them that are in Christ Jesus." Putting it in its positive form, he speaks of being " justified in Christ." Now here we confront a well-known difficulty. We are told that God justifies the ungodly. The term which the apostle uses means " to declare righteous "; it is the opposite of " condemn," as we see from the passage, " It is God that justifieth, who is he that shall condemn ? " Does God, then, declare the ungodly to be righteous ? Does not this statement mean that God declares something to be true wh'ch, as a matter of fact, is false ? This charge of immorality has often been urged against Paul's teaching. I believe, however, that when we have understood it, it really does not lie open to such a criticism. We are not moving in a realm of fiction. Paul's language is paradoxical, but it must be read in the light of his fundamental conception. This is that a man is justified in Christ, that if he is in Christ there is no condemnation for him. But the very fact that the union with Christ has taken place has carried with it the ethical change. The man who is in Christ is a new creature, and it is the new creature who has become such through mystical union with his Saviour who is declared to be righteous. He who was ungodly has now ceased to be so. It is not while he is ungodly before he has become one with Christ that he is so described, but after the union has been effected and he is ungodly no more. Hence we must not wring the last drop of meaning, as some are disposed to do, out of the expression "justifies the ungodly," but recognise that Paul is here using language which, from a popular point of view, excellently expresses his meaning. We should none of us, I presume, object to say that God declares the sinner righteous when he believes in Christ, but we should not wish to be taken to mean that his faith had produced no radical change in his condition. In other words, justification is a result of the mystical union. It holds a secondary and not a primary place in Paul's doctrine of salvation. But it may be said, Does not Paul refer justification to faith as its cause? Certainly he does, but that in no way contradicts the doctrine I have just been expounding. For the union with Christ is itself the result of faith, and since this includes justification, we may speak of God's declaration of innocence as resting either upon union with Christ, which is its immediate, or faith, which is its more remote cause.

We must not be blind to the depth and richness of Paul's conception of faith. It is not the mere recognition that a certain set of historical facts is true, that Jesus of Nazareth died on the Cross and rose again from the dead. Nor is it the acceptance of a theological interpretation of these facts, that they released energies for the salvation of mankind. This coldly intellectual way of regarding them is alien altogether from the evangelical idea of faith. There is intended by it rather a temper and attitude of the soul. It implies as its necessary condition the sinner's consciousness of his condition, of his guilt and moral helplessness, and the impossibility of releasing himself from either one or the other. In this state of condemnation and impotence, finding in himself and in the world about him no relief for his condition, he is prepared to respond to the message of salvation in Christ. Casting away all thought of his own merit as commending him to God, for he feels himself to be a sinner in God's sight, renouncing all efforts at self-reformation as superficial and ineffective, his whole being turns with a glad sense of confidence to Him that is mighty to save, with the deep gratitude of one who has been saved from despair. Cutting himself loose from all the supports on which he has hitherto rested, he takes the supreme risk of faith and launches himself into the void, but he makes his venture in the confidence that he will not be left to his fate, but be caught and held fast by the everlasting arms. And this faith, in which self-surrender, love, gratitude, and implicit trust are mingled, effects the mystical union between the soul and its Saviour. The intellectual element is presupposed in it, the believer must recognise the existence of God, his own sin, and God's

reaction against it, his inability to attain the moral
ideal which God demands from him, the truth of
the great redemptive facts proclaimed in the Gospel.
This is the indispensable foundation of faith. But
faith is something which embraces also the emotions
and the will, it is the movement of the whole personality, the soul's flight for refuge to Christ. Its
inmost mystery, indeed, baffles analysis; how it
effects the mystical union is God's secret and not ours.
But its mystical effect must be closely allied to its
emotional element.

We do a great injustice to religion when we disparage
its emotional quality. It is a danger into which the
quiet and sedate and conventional are particularly
liable to fall, although we must not omit the superior
people whose attitude to life is that of a one-sided
intellectualism. But the student of religion is well
aware how large and decisive a part is played in it by
emotion. And where we are dealing with a God who
is conceived not simply as the philosopher thinks of
Him, but as the Father of spirits whose inmost nature
is love, the religion can be no other than emotional
in character. The term must, of course, be used in no
narrow sense. The expression of emotion depends
very largely on temperament, on external conditions,
on culture. It is not the brawling brook which runs
deepest, and the emotion of the still mystic as he
broods in his cell may be deep and intense to a degree
far surpassing that expressed in noisier demonstration.

The question is not, Do sparks fly off at the surface? but, Does the fire glow hot at the centre? But whether it is in the rapture of the revival service, or in the ecstasy of the mystic's contemplation, the vital thing is that God and the soul should meet, and in the shock of that contact the soul's deepest bliss and satisfaction should be won. The experience hardly lends itself to analysis, but peace is perhaps the best description. The rebel who chose his own will rather than the will of God has laid down his arms and made a complete surrender. And now he enjoys peace with God, from whom he had been estranged. In himself the inward discord has ceased, self has been replaced by Christ. He is no longer distracted between the lower and the higher nature, nor does his better self chafe under the dominion of sin and the flesh.

A new character, as well as a new status, flows inevitably from union with Christ. The flesh has been crucified, and thus sin has lost its fortress within the camp from which it ruled the hapless victim of its tyranny. He is no longer under the Law, he has risen into the freedom of the children of God. He has died with Christ to sin, and in union with Him lives a new life. His life is the expression no longer of the old self, but of Christ, who lives at the very centre of his personality. He is a member of Christ, in immediate contact with the Head, drawing from Him all the supplies of life and power, controlled by Him in thought, word, and action.

Now this representation of the Christian as living a life controlled in every detail by the indwelling Christ appears to be in conflict with experience, inasmuch as even in the Church nothing seems to be rarer than a saint. We can leave aside the case of nominal Christians, whose profession is in flagrant contrast with their life and character. But even the really good people frequently distress us by flaws which are out of harmony with the name they are anxious to adorn. What, then, are we to say on Paul's doctrine in the light of these familiar facts? Paul himself was perfectly aware of them. He was not only a speculative theologian of the highest eminence, but he was a shepherd of souls. He was constantly confronted by difficulties of this very kind. He therefore did not feel that his own doctrine was contradicted by experience. The question is, no doubt, a difficult one, but I believe the solution to be as follows. When Paul is dealing with the subject as a theologian, he treats it from what we may call an ideal or absolute point of view. But he sets before us the principles which he discerns at work as they are in their intrinsic character, not as they are modified in action by other conditions. It is a great advantage for us that he has disengaged these principles from their temporary limitations and suffered us to see the whole Divine drama of salvation in its essential meaning. Ideally sanctification precedes justification, but in experience it is otherwise. I believe that we may plausibly connect this with the strength of faith exercised at the opening of the Christian life. It is normally a feeble faith, which, while it is the promise of all that Paul in his boldest flights describes, yet effects only a rudimentary change. As the Christian life deepens and advances, this faith grows stronger and the union with Christ which it creates more intimate. And, on the other side, the flesh, so deeply seated in the personality, fights desperately for every inch of ground. Thus it is that the real and the ideal so rarely coincide. To the question whether in this world they could coincide, I think that Paul would have answered, " According to your faith be it done unto you."

This union with Christ finds its consummation in the heavenly destiny which it opens up before the believer. However we may speculate on the mysterious problems of the future, in this respect, at least, the Christian can feel no misgiving. By death Jesus escaped from the power of death and can die no more. So those who are one with Him participate in His deathless life. They cannot be less immortal than He is. His existence and theirs are twined together at the roots. Their life is hid with Him in God, but the secret forces which are withdrawn from the gaze of men will be revealed when they enter into possession of their glorious inheritance. It is with no tawdry splendours that we would imagine it bedecked. But all for which the heart most hungers, all to which the pure spirit most aspires, the satisfaction of love's longing, the attainment of the loftiest ideals—these are the saints' inheritance awaiting them in the realm of light.

THE END

PLYMOUTH
WILLIAM BRENDON AND SON, LTD.
PLYMOUTH

Messrs. Duckworth & Co. announce under the title of "Studies in Theology," a new series of handbooks, being aids to interpretation in Biblical Criticism for the use of the Clergy, Divinity Students, and thoughtful Laymen. Crown 8vo, 3s. net.

The aim of the series is described by the general title. It is an attempt to bring the resources of modern learning to the interpretation of the Scriptures and to place within the reach of all who are interested the broad conclusions arrived at by men of distinction in the world of scholarship.

Among the volumes in preparation are the following :—

An Encyclopædia of Theology. By the Rev. A. M. Fairbairn, D.D., D.Litt., LL.D., Principal of Mansfield College, Oxford.

Philosophy and Religion. By the Rev. Hastings Rashdall, D.D.

A Critical Introduction to the Old Testament. By the Rev. George Buchanan Gray, D.D., D.Litt., Professor of Hebrew and Old Testament Exegesis, Mansfield College, Oxford.

A Critical Introduction to the New Testament. By Arthur Samuel Peake, D.D., Professor of Biblical Exegesis and Dean of the Faculty of Theology, Victoria University, Manchester. Sometime Fellow of Merton College, Oxford.

Revelation and Inspiration. By the Rev. James Orr, D.D., Professor of Apologetics in the Theological College of the United Free Church, Glasgow.

Faith and its Psychology. By the Rev. William R. Inge, D.D. Lady Margaret Professor of Divinity, Cambridge, and Bampton Lecturer, Oxford, 1899.

Incarnation and Atonement. By the Rev. James Iverach, D.D., Principal of the United Free Church College, Aberdeen.

History of Christian Thought since Kant. By the Rev. Edward Caldwell Moore, D.D., Parkman Professor of Theology in the University of Harvard, U.S.A.

Other Volumes will in due course be announced.

Duckworth & Co., 3 Henrietta Street, Covent Garden.